Internet English

Teacher's Book

www-based
communication
activities

**Christina Gitsaki &
Richard P. Taylor**

OXFORD
UNIVERSITY PRESS

OXFORD

UNIVERSITY PRESS

198 Madison Avenue, New York, NY 10016 USA
Great Clarendon Street, Oxford OX2 6DP England

Oxford University Press is a department of the University of Oxford. It
furthers the University's objective of excellence in research, scholarship,
and education by publishing worldwide in

Oxford   New York
Athens   Auckland   Bangkok   Bogotá   Buenos Aires   Calcutta
Cape Town   Chennai   Dar es Salaam   Delhi   Florence   Hong Kong
Istanbul   Karachi   Kuala Lumpur   Madrid   Melbourne   Mexico
City   Mumbai   Nairobi   Paris   São Paolo   Singapore   Taipei
Tokyo   Toronto   Warsaw

with associated companies in
Berlin   Ibadan

OXFORD is a registered trademark of Oxford University Press

ISBN 0-19-437227-8

Published in the United States by Oxford University Press, Inc.,
New York

Editor: Chris Foley
Associate Editor: Paul MacIntyre
Production Editor: Anita Raducanu
Editorial Assistant: Maura Tukey
Designer: Tom Hawley, Hawley Design
Production Manager: Abram Hall
Production and Prepress Services: A Plus Publishing Services
Cover Design: Tom Hawley, Hawley Design

Printing (last digit)   10 9 8 7 6 5 4 3

Printed in Hong Kong

Acknowledgements
Pages 21 & 84: Box shots reprinted with permission
    from Microsoft Corporation
Page 87: Courtesy of Blue Mountain Arts

Consultants
Tom Robb
Anthea Tillyer

Contents

WIMBLEDON SCHOOL OF ENGLISH
41 WORPLE ROAD WIMBLEDON
LONDON SW19 4JZ

Scope & Sequence

Unit	Identify	Basic Information	Basic Terminology	Skills Development	Skills Practice
Unit 1 Computers Today	Uses of computers	Computer hardware	Basic computer terminology	Practicing typing, cutting and pasting	Writing an introduction about yourself
Unit 2 Surfing the Web	Things to do on the Web	Internet FAQs	Strategies for searching the Web	Electronic trivia quiz	Comparing search engines
Unit 3 Electronic Mail	Ways of communicating	Free E-mail accounts on the Web	Parts of an E-mail message	Sending and receiving E-mail	Introducing yourself by E-mail

Unit	Identify	Prepare Your Search	Search the Web	Web Talk	Project
Unit 4 Famous People	Famous people and their occupations	Choosing a favorite famous person	Finding information about a famous person	Interviewing a classmate about a famous person	Creating a famous person profile
Unit 5 Web Cards	Types of greeting cards	Preparing to send Web cards	Sending Web cards to classmates	Viewing Web cards; classroom Web card survey	Making and sending greeting cards
Unit 6 Study Abroad	Reasons for studying abroad	Choosing an English language study course	Researching English language programs	Scholarship interview	Creating a school brochure
Unit 7 Eating Out	Types of international foods	Choosing a type of restaurant and food	Locating websites of restaurants with menus	Role-play: Ordering food at a restaurant	Creating a restaurant brochure
Unit 8 Shopping Spree	Ways of shopping	Choosing things to buy online	Finding items in online shopping catalogs	Discussing shopping experiences	Creating a shopping catalog page
Unit 9 Watching Movies	Movie ratings and preferences	Discussing movies and deciding on one to research	Finding information about movies	Interviewing a classmate about a movie	Advertising a movie
Unit 10 Vacation Abroad	Vacation preferences	Planning a vacation abroad: destinations and activities	Researching vacation information	Interviewing a classmate about vacation plans	Advertising a vacation
Unit 11 Cyber C@fes	Things to do at cyber cafes	Discussing cyber cafes and deciding on one to research	Researching cyber cafes	Interviewing a classmate about a cyber cafe	Advertising a cyber cafe
Unit 12 Working Abroad	Jobs and workplaces	Reviewing skills and qualities; choosing a job to research	Finding jobs on databases	Role-play: Job interview	Advertising a job
Unit 13 News Online	Ways to get the news	Reading and talking about a news story	Finding and reading a news story	Interviewing a classmate about a news story	Summarizing a news story

Introduction

Internet English is a WWW-based conversation course for pre-intermediate and intermediate learners. It allows students to pursue their particular preferences and interests through the use of the Internet as a classroom resource.

This approach has many advantages:

- The Internet provides students with opportunities for exposure to natural language and authentic language use not only during but also outside the class, making learning English part of students' daily lives and an ongoing process.

- The Internet offers a variety of topics to satisfy a diverse audience.

- The information available on the Internet is current and frequently updated.

- Using the Internet is fun and highly motivating. Websites are full of animation, colors, sounds, pictures, interactive forms, and digital video clips.

- Using the Internet has become a part of life and learning how to use it is an essential skill for students. Through the use of *Internet English*, students develop basic information technology (IT) skills (e.g., word processing skills, Web-browsing skills, E-mail skills) and learn English at the same time.

- Using the Internet for English language teaching and learning enhances student autonomy and gives learners the opportunity to manage their own learning.

The Internet offers a wealth of information and unlimited resources that teachers can use in order to expose students to authentic language use. Exposure, however, is not enough to best facilitate language acquisition. Students need to be involved in tasks that integrate the use of computers, the Internet, and language acquisition. *Internet English* comprises carefully designed *Web Search* units that involve students in meaningful language tasks. Each *Web Search* unit introduces students to a topic and gives them some guidance to help

them with the language they will encounter. Then students are left on their own to direct their learning to the areas they are interested in. In this respect, students are in charge of their learning and able to direct themselves to language resources that are appealing to them.

Internet English Course Components

Internet English - Student Book

- 13 four-page units comprising 3 *Computer Skills* units and 10 *Web Search* units

- 13 *Practice Pages (Language Window, Computer Project, Share Your Project)*

- 3 *Technical Tips* pages

- An *Internet Vocabulary* glossary

Internet English - Teacher's Book

- Step-by-step instructions for each unit

- Answer keys to activities

- An *Extension Activity* for each unit

- Lists of useful URLs related to the topic of each unit

- A *Vocabulary Log*

- An *Introduction to HTML* showing students how to create an English language homepage

- Four tests

Internet English Website

- Student Keypal Center

- Teacher WWW-Board

- Useful URLs for each unit in the **Student Book**

- Links to websites concerned with English language teaching and learning

Lesson Planning

Internet English consists of 13 four-page units. Units 1–3 are *Computer Skills* units aimed at introducing students to basic word-processing, E-mail and Web searching skills. Units 4–13 are *Web Search* units to be taught either in a computer lab or in a traditional classroom. A typical *Web Search* unit has four sections: the *Identify* section with visual stimuli and warm up activities; the *Prepare Your Search* section for vocabulary building and narrowing down ideas and preferences in preparation for the Web search task; the *Search the Web* section guides students through their Web search and collection of specific information; the *Web Talk* section where students are involved in speaking tasks for sharing the information they found on the Web. Each unit also includes a *Practice Page* with a language structure activity and a computer project that students can share via E-mail.

A class using *Internet English* can be structured in a variety of ways. It contains enough material for approximately 40 classroom hours. This number may vary according to the instructor's teaching style and the individual goals of the class. A sample lesson plan for the traditional and computer-equipped classroom cases follow. Both lesson plans assume 90-minute class sessions.

In a Computer Lab

Each *Web Search* unit can be taught over two sessions.

Session 1. Students complete the *Identify* and *Prepare Your Search* sections. The *Language Window* is introduced and the writing activity given as homework. Students write down their set of keywords for their Web search and then use the computers for the *Search the Web* section.

Session 2. After completing the *Search the Web* section, students carry out the *Web Talk*. Students then use their computers to put together the *Computer Project* and then E-mail it to some of their classmates.

In a Traditional Classroom

In a traditional classroom, the computer activities are carried out by students outside of class as homework. Each *Web Search* unit can be taught over two sessions.

Session 1. Students complete the *Identify* and *Prepare Your Search* sections. They also write

down the keywords for their Web search. The Web search is given as homework to be completed outside the class, in a computer lab or using a personal computer. Students are also asked to print out some of the information and pictures from their Web search and bring the printouts to class for Session 2. The *Language Window* is introduced and its writing activity completed in class. Students can also work on the *Extension Activity* related to the topic of the unit as outlined in the **Teacher's Book**.

Session 2. Students come to class with the results of their Web search and they carry out the *Web Talk*. If students have no access to a computer during class, then the *Computer Project* can be carried out as a classroom project. Students use pictures and information from the Web and put together a project. They then post their projects in class and share them with their classmates. Alternatively, the *Computer Project* can be completed outside the class, before Session 2. During Session 2, students can make classroom or group presentations of their projects.

Structure of the Teacher's Book

Each unit in the **Teacher's Book** consists of four pages of instructions for carrying out the activities in the **Student Book**, *Teaching Tips* and *Web Tips*, and optional activities; a photocopiable *Extension Activity*; and one page with a list of useful URLs related to the topic of the unit. The **Teacher's Book** also contains a photocopiable *Vocabulary Log* to be used with each unit, four photocopiable tests for assessing students, and a photocopiable *Introduction to HTML* for helping your students create an English language homepage in basic HTML.

Classroom Management and Logistics

Teaching in a computer lab

Internet English is designed to be used with any type of computer that has Web access. Before teaching in a computer lab, you will need to make sure that there is one computer per student. You will also need to make sure that each computer in the lab has access to the Internet, has a Web browser (e.g., Netscape™, Internet Explorer™), and a word processor (e.g., Claris Works™, Microsoft Word™, Word Perfect™). If possible, obtain English language software to use with your students. This way students get used to using computer terms in English. In many schools, students need a password in order to access the computers in a lab. You may have to find out this information before your first *Internet English* lesson. Furthermore, you may need to establish classroom rules for your students to follow. Here are some things to consider.

- It is a good idea to keep computers shut down until it is time for carrying out computer tasks (e.g., searching the Web for specific information). Have students turn on their computer only when you ask them to complete certain tasks.

- Ask students to make copies of the files they create on a floppy disk and make sure to take their floppy with them at the end of the lesson.

- Finally, students should be responsible for quitting all applications and shutting down their computer at the end of the lesson.

Pair Work and Group Work

A lot of the activities in the book require students to work in pairs or groups. It is a good idea to explain to students that working with their classmates is very beneficial for them. It provides opportunities to exchange ideas, compare answers, and practice conversations. You may also suggest that students work with different classmates instead of working with the same classmate repeatedly. If you are teaching in a computer lab, you may find that students are inclined to look at their computer screen at all times. This is because in a regular computer class, students usually use the computer on their own and there is little or no interaction with other classmates. However, the primary goal of *Internet English* is not to teach computers. Rather, it is a conversation course that utilizes computers and the Internet. Therefore, you will need to clarify to students from the start of the semester that they are expected to do a lot of pair work and group work in class, and that they should be prepared to stand up and find a partner or form groups at any time during the lesson. Regarding space for moving around, most computer labs have corridors and space at the back of the room or the front of the room. If space in your lab is limited, you can do pair work by asking students to work with the person next to

them (in labs where students sit in pairs), or to turn and work with the classmate behind them (in labs where students sit back to back). In a traditional classroom, you should have no problem moving students around and having students form groups or pairs.

Printing

Some activities require printing Web pages or projects. One major concern when a whole class sends files to the printer at the same time is that there may be a file jam. To avoid such jams, have students send their files to the printer in groups of 10 or less. In some schools, students are expected to pay a small fee or bring their own paper for printing their projects. You may have to ask your school about their policy. If there is no printer in the lab, students will have to do their printing outside classroom time.

E-mailing Attachments

The E-mail tasks in *Internet English* are mainly for exchanging information electronically (i.e., in the *Share Your Project* section of the **Student Book,** students are asked to E-mail their computer writing project to a group of 3–4 students). You will need to show students how to E-mail attachments and how to open the attached files. If you would like your students to exchange E-mail with other students from different parts of the world (i.e., keypals), ask students to post a message in the Student Keypal Center of the *Internet English Website.* They can browse through messages posted by other students from other schools and choose a couple of keypals to send E-mail to. If the keypals are from the same country as your students, encourage your students to use English when they write E-mail to their keypals. You may also want to direct your students to other websites designed to help English language learners find keypals (see list of useful ESL sites in the *Internet English Website*). Explain to your students that having a keypal is their responsibility. They are responsible for replying to E-mail messages and keeping their keypal, and they should not wait until they come to your class to check their E-mail and write E-mail messages to their keypals.

Computer Hardware Troubleshooting

There are no specific hardware problems that can arise from the use of the computers with the

Internet English activities. However, computer hardware problems may occur due to regular wear and tear. Therefore, should you need help, you will want to make sure you have access to your school's computer technician.

Computer Software Troubleshooting

Although you do not need to be a computer wizard to teach *Internet English,* it is necessary to familiarize yourself with the software that your students and you will need to use for searching the Web, doing the computer projects and using E-mail. You need to know these basic operations:

- **word processing:** opening a new file, cutting and pasting information, saving files, printing files
- **Web surfing:** opening a Web browser, typing keywords, browsing through search results, clicking on links, going forward and back, adding bookmarks, copying and pasting information and images from the Web to a word processing document
- **E-mail:** opening the E-mailer, composing an E-mail message, sending E-mail and attachments, reading and replying to E-mail, saving and deleting E-mail messages

Occasionally, things will go wrong, but as long as you and your students make backup copies of the files you are working on, the losses should be minimal. Remind students to bring a floppy disk with them for saving their files.

Finding Information on the Web

Internet portals (i.e., websites with search engines and Web directories) are very sophisticated nowadays and able to find information on any topic instantly. In the **Student Book** the first activity in the *Search the Web* section is dedicated to helping students sort out their keywords before their search. Having a clear set of keywords can save a lot of time when searching for specific information on the Web. It is not uncommon for a search engine to return tens of thousands of entries for a single search. This is not a concern, as long as you and your students can find one or two relevant sites among the first 10 entries. If any of your students are unable to find a relevant site, you can direct them to one or several of the suggested URLs listed in every unit of the **Teacher's Book** and at the *Internet English Website.*

Assessment

For assessing and grading your students we have included four 50-point tests in the **Teacher's Book.** Each test is to be used after the completion of a specific set of units. They test a range of computer skills, language structures and vocabulary that students have been exposed to when carrying out the activities in the **Student Book.** In addition, you may also want to grade your students' project work. Have them print out their projects and submit them to you at the end of each unit. When grading students' projects, here are a few things to keep in mind: remind students to credit all the URLs they used in order to get information and pictures for their project. Students should be careful not to just copy and paste text from the Web, but to edit, paraphrase and modify copied information. Ask students to keep the amount of images they include in their project to the minimum; otherwise you may find students submitting pages upon pages of images with very little content. List a few general points of formatting that you would like your students to follow, e.g., put a title in large font size, include the list of URLs at the end of the document, include the student name and number at the bottom of each page, check the spelling before printing. You may find that the more proficient students include more of their ideas and thoughts in their projects while the less proficient students tend to copy most of the information included in their projects with very little editing or personal contributions. Finally, you may want to arrange for students to make class presentations of their projects (2–3 presentations per lesson depending on your class size).

Teacher Support

If you have any questions, comments, ideas on any of the activities in *Internet English,* you can post them on the *Internet English Website* (Teacher WWW-board). The purpose of the Teacher WWW-board is to offer support to teachers using *Internet English* and to respond to their questions online.

UNIT 1 Computers Today

IDENTIFY STUDENT BOOK, page 2	Uses of computers
COMPUTER HARDWARE STUDENT BOOK, page 3	Basic parts of a computer
COMPUTER TERMS STUDENT BOOK, page 4	Computer terms and definitions
COMPUTER PRACTICE STUDENT BOOK, page 5	Unscramble a story: Using Cut and Paste functions Word processing practice
PRACTICE PAGE STUDENT BOOK, page 55	Language Window—Unscrambling instructions on how to Cut and Paste Computer Project—Write a self-introduction

KEY VOCABULARY

actress	DOS	keyboard	Save
arrow	dot	MacOS™	schoolwork
asleep	dreadful	menu	scrambled
brand	E-mail	monitor	screen
CD-ROM	edit	mouse	shift
CD-ROM drive	escape (esc)	Netscape™	slash
click	executive producer	Open	space bar
Close	file	operating system	surf the Web
colon	floppy disk	parenthesis	symbol
comma	floppy disk drive	Paste	tab
control (ctrl)	freeway	perform	unscrambled
Copy	hardware	performance	Web browser
crowded	highlight	period	window
cursor	hyphen	preserve	Windows
Cut	icon	Print	word processor
dash	image	rehearsal	
delete	Internet Explorer™	release	
document	key	return (enter)	

INTRODUCTION

1. Introduce the unit to students. Tell them that this unit is about using computers.
2. Now ask students to open their books. Outline the sequence of activities. Tell students that first they will identify different uses of computers in their life; then they will review the different parts of a computer and the keyboard; after that they will familiarize themselves with some basic computer and word processing terms and their definitions; and finally, they will explore and practice some basic computer operations.

PHOTO WARM-UP

PAGE 2

Ask students to have a look at the picture of a young woman at a computer. Ask students questions related to the picture. For example, ask students:

- *Where is the woman?*
- *What is she doing?*
- *Have you used a computer before?*
- *Do you have a computer at home?*

IDENTIFY

PAGE 2

1. Review the different uses of computers with students and ask them to circle what they like to use computers for.

2. Ask students to write two more ideas in the chart.

PAIR WORK: When students have finished writing, ask them to compare their answers with a classmate using the model dialog for guidance.

OPTIONAL

Take some time to ask students about what they like to use computers for. For example, ask individual students:

- *How often do you use a computer?*
- *Who likes to use a computer for sending E-mail?*
- *Who likes to use a computer for writing letters?*

COMPUTER HARDWARE

PAGE 3

1. Direct students' attention to the picture of the computer. Review the *Computer Hardware* terms in the box.

2. Ask students to write each of the words from the box in the correct space.

3. Ask students to compare their answers with a classmate's.

ANSWERS

1. Screen/Monitor
2. CD-ROM
3. Floppy Disk
4. Floppy Disk Drive
5. CD-ROM drive
6. Keyboard
7. Mouse

OPTIONAL

After students have completed identifying the parts of the computer, ask them to tell you their answers aloud. For example, point to each computer part in the picture (or a real computer if you have a computer in the classroom) and ask students what each part is called.

1. Students can answer questions 1 to 5 for a computer in front of them or from memory about the computer they usually use. Question 6 should be answered in front of a computer.

2. After they finish, students can compare their answers with a partner's.

OPTIONAL

After students have finished section B, check their answers aloud in class. For example, ask students:

- *What brand is your computer?*
- *What is the operating system of your computer?*

EXTENSION ACTIVITY

COMPUTER SURVEY

1. Photocopy the *Extension Activity* on page 5 of the **Teacher's Book.** Make one copy for each student.

2. Ask students to find a partner. For each item, students ask their partner question *a*. If their partner answers "No" to the question, they move on to the next question. If their partner answers "Yes" they need to ask question *b* (a follow-up question) and write down their partner's answer.

COMPUTER TERMS

PAGE 4

Ask students to match the word-processing terms with their definitions. Then have them compare their answers with a classmate's.

ANSWERS

1. menu
2. window
3. icon
4. file (document)
5. word processor
6. click
7. cursor
8. highlight

OPTIONAL

After students have finished **A**, check their answers aloud in class. For example, ask students:

- *What does "click" mean?*
- *What is "highlight"?*

Now ask students to match the word-processing commands with their definitions. Then have them compare their answers with a classmate's.

ANSWERS

1. Copy
2. Save
3. Cut and Paste
4. Open
5. New
6. Print
7. Close
8. Save As

OPTIONAL

After students have finished **B**, check their answers in class. For example, ask students:

- *What does "New" mean?*
- *What is "Print"?*

TEACHING TIP

As you check students' answers in class and review the definitions, explain any unfamiliar vocabulary and make sure students understand what each term means. If you are teaching this in a computer lab, use a computer to exemplify the word-processing terms and commands.

LANGUAGE WINDOW

At this point it is a good idea to introduce the *Language Window* to students (see page 55 of the **Student Book** or page 4 of the **Teacher's Book**).

COMPUTER PRACTICE

PAGE 5

Ask students to open their word-processing software and type the sentences in **A** in a new text file. When they have finished, ask them to save the text file as *Scrambled*.

Ask students to read the scrambled story in *A* and then put the sentences in the correct order (ask them to number the sentences 1–11 in their book).

Ask students to put the sentences in the correct order in the text file by highlighting the sentences, cutting, and pasting the text.

1. When they have finished ordering the sentences, ask them to save the file as *Unscrambled*.
2. If possible ask students to make a printout of their unscrambled story. It maybe useful to organize students to take turns when printing their projects to avoid printing jams.

ANSWERS

11, 3, 10, 4, 5, 1, 6, 7, 8, 2, 9

E PAIR WORK: Have students exchange stories with a partner and read their partner's story. Students should confirm that their stories are the same, or discuss any differences.

> **TEACHING TIP**
>
> This activity serves a dual goal: it helps students practice typing and performing basic word-processing operations (e.g., cut, paste, highlight, save). Therefore, it is important to have students type the sentences themselves.

IN A TRADITIONAL CLASSROOM

If you are teaching *Internet English* in a classroom without computers, students can do the *Computer Practice* partly in class and partly for homework:

1. Ask students to read the scrambled sentences in **A** and then put them in the correct order (ask them to number the sentences 1–13 on their book).
2. Ask students to compare their story with a classmate, in groups or with the rest of the class.
3. Give students instructions for re-ordering the sentences on the computer for homework.

LANGUAGE WINDOW

PAGE 55

A. Review the scrambled instructions in the *Language Window*.
B. Ask students to write the instructions in the correct order. This can also be given as homework if there is not enough time during the lesson.
C. Ask students to compare their answers with a classmate's. You can also review students' answers in class.

> **ANSWERS**
>
> 1. First, highlight the information you want to move.
> 2. Next, select Cut from the Edit menu
> 3. Then, move the cursor to the new place on the screen.
> 4. Finally, select Paste from the Edit menu.

COMPUTER PROJECT

PAGE 55

1. PROJECT: Ask students to create a self-introduction using their word processor. Show them the sample self-introduction in the book. Ask students to include the following and anything else they would like to share with their classmates:

   - Title
   - Personal Information: name, age, hometown, hobbies, etc.
   - Why they are learning English

2. Ask students to save the file as *YourName*.Introduction.
3. If possible ask students to make a printout of their self-introduction. It may be useful to organize students to take turns when printing their projects to avoid printing jams.

SHARE YOUR PROJECT

PAGE 55

1. Ask students to have a look at a classmate's self-introduction and then answer the question in their book.
2. Ask students to share their answer with another classmate.

IN A TRADITIONAL CLASSROOM

If you are teaching *Internet English* in a classroom without computers, you can ask students to create their self-introduction in class without using computers:

1. Ask students to bring a picture of themselves, a glue stick, color markers, and a blank piece of paper or poster board to class.
2. Ask students to create a self-introduction. Ask them to paste their picture on the blank paper or poster board, and then use the color markers to write some information about themselves.
3. When students have finished their self-introduction, they can post it in class.

COMPUTER SURVEY

PAIR WORK. For 1–8 below, first ask question *a* to your partner. If he/she answers "Yes," ask question *b* and write down his/her answer.

Questions	Answers
1a. Do you have a computer at home? **b.** What kind of computer do you have?	**1a.** ☐ Yes ☐ No **b.** _____
2a. Do you want a new computer? **b.** What kind of computer do you want?	**2a.** ☐ Yes ☐ No **b.** _____
3a. Do you like to play computer games? **b.** What computer games do you like to play?	**3a.** ☐ Yes ☐ No **b.** _____
4a. Do you use E-mail? **b.** How often do you use E-mail?	**4a.** ☐ Yes ☐ No **b.** _____
5a. Do you think computers are important for students? **b.** Why do you think computers are important for students?	**5a.** ☐ Yes ☐ No **b.** _____
6a. Do you want a job that uses computers? **b.** What kind of job do you want?	**6a.** ☐ Yes ☐ No **b.** _____
7a. Can you use at least three types of software? **b.** What types of software can you use?	**7a.** ☐ Yes ☐ No **b.** _____
8a. Do you ever surf the Web? **b.** What websites do you visit?	**8a.** ☐ Yes ☐ No **b.** _____

Go To: `file:///www`

1. **MaranGraphics Computer Dictionary:** Dictionary of computer terms with explanations and 3D illustrations.

    http://207.136.90.76/dictionary/

2. **Garelochead Computer Club Online:** Introduction to the parts of a computer with pictures and short descriptions.

    http://www.tzone.demon.co.uk/comintro.htm

3. **Whatis.com:** Directory of explanatory pages on computers, word processing, and the Internet.

    http://www.whatis.com/index.htm

4. **Matisse's Glossary of Internet Terms:** Glossary of Internet and computer terms.

    http://www.matisse.net/files/glossary.html#C

5. **Types of Word Processing Programs:** Webpage with useful information on word processors.

    http://klingon.cs.iupui.edu/~aharris/mmcc/mod3/abwp1.html

6. **Nerd World Media:** A comprehensive directory of computer companies.

    http://www.nerdworld.com/nw368.html

7. **Virtual Computer History Museum:** Pages on the history of the computer with pictures and text.

    http://video.cs.vt.edu:90/cgi-bin/TicketWindow?DejaVu=Yes

8. **History in the Computing Curriculum:** A website created by John Impagliazzo, contains a chronology and other useful links.

    http://www.hofstra.edu/Communities/frame.html?bounce=/ComputingHistory/

9. **Early Typewriter History:** History of the keyboard.

    http://www.mit.edu/~jcb/Dvorak/history.html

Add your favorite websites for this unit here:

1. _____
2. _____
3. _____
4. _____

UNIT 2 Surfing the Web

IDENTIFY STUDENT BOOK, page 6	Things to do on the Web
INTRO TO THE INTERNET STUDENT BOOK, page 7	Frequently asked questions about the Internet
WEB SEARCH ENGINES STUDENT BOOK, page 8	Strategies for searching the Web Search operators
ELECTRONIC TRIVIA QUIZ STUDENT BOOK, page 9	Game: Electronic Trivia Quiz
PRACTICE PAGE STUDENT BOOK, page 56	Language Window–Wh-questions Comparing search engines

KEY VOCABULARY

business	Internet	order	supercomputer
cable	keyword	personal	symbol
CEO	limit	phrase	travel plans
connection	link	research	trivia
contain	magazine	satellite	URL
defense	meal	search engine	Web
entertainment	microwave	search operator	Web page
fiberoptic	military	shopping	website
high-speed	network	specific	World Wide Web

INTRODUCTION

1. Introduce the topic to students. Tell them that this unit is about the Internet, the World Wide Web, and how to search the Web for specific information.

2. Now ask students to open their books. Outline the sequence of activities. Tell students that first they will identify different things to do on the Web; then they will read some information about the Internet; after that they will learn how to use a search engine; and finally they will play an electronic trivia game.

PHOTO WARM-UP

PAGE 6

Ask students to have a look at the picture. Ask them questions about the picture. For example, ask students:

- *What do you think these students are doing?*

- *What kind of computer are they using?*

- *Have you surfed the Web before?*

- *What kind of information did you search for?*

- *Do you like surfing the Web? Why or why not?*

PAGE 6

 A

Review the list of things to do on the Web. Ask students to check **yes** or **no** to indicate which things they would like to do on the Web. Then have students add one more item to the list.

TEACHING TIP

You may need to explain some of the things mentioned in section **A**. For example: "meet people" refers to having keypals, video conferencing, joining chat rooms, etc.; "get the latest news" through online news services; "order a meal" or food through a website; "find a job" by searching job databases; "go shopping" using online shopping malls; "make travel plans" finding information about airfares, hotels, holiday activities.

 B

PAIR WORK: When students have finished writing, ask them to compare their answers with a classmate's using the model dialog for guidance.

OPTIONAL

Take some time to ask students about the things they checked. For example, ask students:

- *Who would like to meet people on the Web?*
- *Who would like to get the latest news on the Web?*

INTRODUCTION TO THE INTERNET

PAGE 7

 A

Ask students to read the FAQs about the Internet. You can pre-teach some of the vocabulary or alternatively ask students to use their dictionary.

 B

After students have finished reading, ask them to answer the questions about the Internet.

 C

Have students check their answers with a partner.

ANSWERS

1. They are linked together by telephone lines, fiberoptic cables, satellite, and microwave connections.
2. The United States Department of Defense in 1969.
3. It looks like a magazine page.
4. Send E-mail, go shopping, find jobs, get the latest news, order a meal, and make travel plans.

OPTIONAL

After students have finished writing, ask individual students to read their answers aloud in class.

LANGUAGE WINDOW

It is a good idea to introduce the *Language Window* to students (see page 56 of the **Student Book** and page 10 of the **Teacher's Book**).

EXTENSION ACTIVITY

WEB DIRECTORY

1. Photocopy the *Extension Activity* on page 11 of the **Teacher's Book**. Make one copy per student.
2. Explain what a Web directory is, and go through the topics and sub-topics in the box. Make sure students understand what the topics and sub-topics mean.
3. Tell students to carefully read each situation (1–8) and choose the best topic and sub-topic for their search.
4. Ask students to compare their answers with a classmate's.

ANSWERS

1. Recreation & Sports: Sports
2. Reference: Dictionaries
3. Recreation & Sports: Travel
4. Entertainment: Humor
5. Health: Nutrition
6. Computers & Internet: Games
7. Business & Economy: Jobs
8. Arts & Humanities: Literature

INTRODUCTION TO URLS

1. Photocopy the *Extension Activity* on page 12 of the **Teacher's Book.** Make one copy per student.

2. Ask students to read the Introduction to URLs. Alternatively, present the Introduction to URLs to the class. Answer any questions students may have.

3. Tell students to complete the matching exercise.

ANSWERS

1.	f	5.	g
2.	h	6.	d
3.	a	7.	e
4.	b	8.	c

4. Ask students to compare their answers with a classmate's.

HOW TO USE A WEB SEARCH ENGINE

PAGE 8

PREPARATION: Go through the explanation of how a search engine works with students. Use the examples in the book to show students how to use keywords.

Review the list of search operators, the example keywords, and search results with students.

Ask students to do the multiple choice activity. Ask them to read each example situation and choose the best keyword for each situation.

ANSWERS

1. b	2. c	3. a	4. a

OPTIONAL

After students have finished the multiple choice activity, check their answers in class.

ELECTRONIC TRIVIA QUIZ

PAGE 9

PREPARATION: Inform students that they will play an electronic trivia game. Review the questions in the book and then ask students to pair up with a classmate and write three more questions. Tell students that they shouldn't know the answers to the questions.

TEACHING TIP

Walk around the classroom and have a look at students' questions. Make sure the questions are suitable for performing Web searches like the examples in the book. Tell students to avoid questions that cannot be answered on the Web, such as "How old is my father?", etc.

After students have finished writing their questions, ask them to write down the keywords they are going to use to search for answers to their questions. Tell them to review the search operators on page 8 of the **Student Book**.

TEACHING TIP

Walk around the classroom and check students' keywords. Make sure they are spelled correctly.

 NOW STUDENTS WILL USE THEIR COMPUTER AND START SEARCHING THE WEB.

Ask students to open their browser and go to a search engine (see *Technical Tips*, page 68 of the **Student Book** for a list of URLs for Internet portals containing search engines and directories on the Web), type in their keywords and then search the Web. Ask students to browse through the results and explore the websites for the answers to their questions.

Ask students to write down the answers to their questions. Students should do the Web search individually (i.e., not with their partner).

E

Ask students to check their answers with their
partner.

OPTIONAL

If you have time you can ask students to share
some of their questions and answers with the rest
of the class.

LANGUAGE WINDOW

PAGE 56

A. Review the examples of wh-questions in the
Language Window.

B. Ask students to write their examples of wh-
questions. This can also be given as homework
if there is not enough time during the lesson.
Review students' questions and/or ask them to
compare their answers with a classmate's.

COMPARING SEARCH ENGINES

PAGE 56

A. Ask students to write the names of some of
the search engines that they know of.

B. Ask students to choose one of the questions
from the *Language Window* and then find the
answer to the question using three different
search engines. After they finish their search
ask them to answer the questions in their book.

C. Finally, ask students to share their answers
with a classmate.

IN A TRADITIONAL CLASSROOM

If you are teaching *Internet English* in a
classroom without computers, you can do the
Electronic Trivia Quiz in class.

1. At the end of the first session, explain the
Electronic Trivia Quiz to students. Ask them
to write down their questions and then
search the Web for the answers to their
questions outside the class.

2. When students come back for the second
session, ask them to write their questions on
a piece of paper and then give two possible
answers to each question (one answer
should be correct and the other answer
should be wrong). If you want to use the
proposed questionnaire form on page 13 of
the **Teacher's Book,** make one copy per
student.

3. Ask students to find a partner and ask each
other their trivia questions. The person who
answers the most questions correctly is the
winner. Tell students to repeat the quiz with
as many partners as time allows.

4. At the end of the game ask students to share
some of their questions and answers in class.

5. You can also ask students which were their
most difficult questions, and which were the
easiest questions.

Surfing the Web
Extension Activity

A *Web directory* is a collection of links to Web pages, arranged by topics and sub-topics.
Look at the Web directory below, then complete the exercise.

Arts & Humanities Literature, Photography…	**Education** Colleges and Universities…	**News & Media** Headlines, Newspapers, TV…
Business & Economy Companies, Finance, Jobs…	**Entertainment** Movies, Humor, Music…	**Recreation & Sports** Sports, Travel, Auto, Outdoors…
Computers & Internet WWW, Software, Games…	**Health** Medicine, Nutrition, Fitness…	**Reference** Libraries, Dictionaries…

A Which topic would you click on in the following situations? Choose a topic (large type) and a sub-topic (small type).

1. You want information about World Cup soccer.

   _____

2. You need to find the meaning of a word in English.

   _____

3. You are planning a trip to Brazil and are looking for travel information.

   _____

4. You are feeling a little unhappy today and you would like to read a good joke.

   _____

5. You are interested in healthy foods.

   _____

6. You want to find out about new computer games.

   _____

7. You need to find a new job.

   _____

8. Your favorite writer has just written a new book, and you would like to know more about it.

   _____

B Compare your answers with a classmate's.

INTRODUCTION TO URLS

A Read the introduction to URLs below.

Introduction to URLs

A **URL** (Universal Resource Locator) is the address of a Web page on the World Wide Web. By typing this in the *Location* window in Netscape or in the *Address* window in Internet Explorer, you can visit the website. Most URLs on the World Wide Web begin:

http://www.
(h-t-t-p-colon-slash-slash-w-w-w-dot)

For many businesses, the URL includes a shortened name of the business plus the ending, **.com** or **.co.** For example, the URL of Apple Computer Corporation is:

http://www.apple.com

For many universities, the URL includes a shortened name of the university plus the ending, **.edu** or **.ac.** For example, the URL for Harvard University is:

http://www.harvard.edu

For countries outside the United States, a *country code* is sometimes added at the end of the URL, e.g., au = Australia, ca = Canada, jp = Japan, kr = South Korea, br = Brazil. (For additional country codes, see *What's in an E-Mail Address* on page 70 of your **Student Book.**)

B Match the companies and universities on the left with their URLs on the right.

Companies and Universities	URLs
1. ☐ The University of Sydney	a. http://www.acer.com
2. ☐ Yamaha Music Corporation	b. http://www.auckland.ac.nz
3. ☐ Acer Electronics	c. http://www.vuitton.com
4. ☐ The University of Auckland	d. http://www.jcrew.com
5. ☐ Oxford University Press	e. http://www.singaporeair.com
6. ☐ J.Crew	f. http://www.usyd.edu.au
7. ☐ Singapore Airlines	g. http://www.oup.com
8. ☐ Louis Vuitton	h. http://www.yamaha.co.jp

Surfing the Web
Electronic Trivia Quiz

**For use with Student Book, page 9,
in a traditional classroom.**

A Write down your five questions. For each question, write down two possible answers (one correct answer and one incorrect answer). Remember to vary the order of the possible answers (don't always put the correct answer first!), and try to make the incorrect answer similar to the correct one.

Example: What is the largest country in the world by area?

a. (Russia)
b. Canada

Questions	Answers
1. _____ _____	1 a. _____ b. _____
2. _____ _____	2 a. _____ b. _____
3. _____ _____	3 a. _____ b. _____
4. _____ _____	4 a. _____ b. _____
5. _____ _____	5 a. _____ b. _____

B Now find a partner and ask each other your questions. The person who answers the most questions correctly is the winner. Repeat with as many partners as time allows.

Go To: `file:///www|`

1. **Glossaries of Internet Terms**
   http://www.nw-direct.com/web_dict.htm
   http://www0.delphi.com/navnet/glossary/index.html
   http://www.matisse.net/files/glossary.html

2. **How the Internet Works**
   http://www.whatis.com/tour.htm

3. **History of the World Wide Web**
   http://ei.cs.vt.edu/book/chap1/net_hist.html

4. **Hobbe's Internet Timeline**
   http://www.isoc.org/guest/zakon/Internet/History/HIT.html

5. **Internet Help:** Links to websites which provide help to new Internet users.
   http://www.city.grande-prairie.ab.ca/h_html.htm

6. **Newbie.net:** A cyber-course introducing beginners to a range of Internet activities.
   http://www.newbie.net/

7. **Learn the Net:** An introduction to the Internet basics.
   http://www.learnthenet.com/english/section/intbas.html

8. **Internet 101:** The basics about the Internet and the World Wide Web.
   http://www2.famvid.com/i101/internet101.html

9. **Beginner's Guide to the Internet:** Links to Internet-related websites for beginners.
   http://www.pbs.org/uti/begin.html

10. **The Internet for Beginners:** The Internet: What is it? Why use it? Internet terminology. What is Netiquette? Search Engines. Resources.
    http://sen.wiu.edu/newbies/intronet.html

Add your favorite websites for this unit here:

1. _____

2. _____

3. _____

4. _____

5. _____

UNIT 3 Electronic Mail

IDENTIFY STUDENT BOOK, page 10	Ways of communicating
E–MAIL ON THE INTERNET STUDENT BOOK, page 11	Create a free E-mail account on the Web
PARTS OF AN E–MAIL STUDENT BOOK, page 12	Parts of an E-mail message E-mail terms and definitions
E–MAIL PRACTICE STUDENT BOOK, page 13	Write and send an E-mail message
PRACTICE PAGE STUDENT BOOK, page 57	E-mail Activity—Use E-mail to find out information about classmates

KEY VOCABULARY

account	E-mail address	recipient
attach	emoticon	registration form
attachment	fax	specify
badminton	format	subject
bcc:	have in common	To:
cc:	message	typical
communicate	password	username
draft	receive	video phone
E–mail		

INTRODUCTION

1. Introduce the topic to students. Tell them that this unit is about electronic mail (E-mail), i.e., using the Internet for sending messages to people.

2. Now ask students to open their books. Outline the sequence of activities. Tell students that first they will talk about different ways of communicating; then they will create an E-mail account on the Internet; after that they will identify the different parts of an E-mail message; and finally they will practice sending and receiving E-mail messages.

WEB PAGE WARM-UP

PAGE 10

Ask students to have a look at the Hotmail graphic. Tell them to read the message. Now ask questions about the E-mail message. For example, ask students:

- *Who is sending this message?*
- *Who is the recipient of the message?*
- *What is the message about?*
- *Do you think E-mail is useful?*

IDENTIFY

PAGE 10

A

Review the different ways of communicating. Ask students to write down how often they use each of these ways of communicating using the frequency expressions from the box or ones of their own.

B

PAIR WORK: When students have finished writing, ask them to compare their answers with a classmate using the model dialog for guidance.

OPTIONAL

Take some time to ask students about their answers. For example, ask students:

• *How often do you write letters?*
• *How often do you talk on the phone?*

E-MAIL ON THE INTERNET

PAGE 11

A

PREPARATION: Tell students that they will look for a free E-mail account on the Web. Tell them to use "free" and "E-mail" as keywords for their search (show them the example in the book). Then tell students that they will explore a few websites that offer free E-mail accounts, choose the one they like the most, and write down the website name and URL. Review the example registration form on page 11, and tell students that they will need to fill in a similar form in order to create their free E-mail account.

EXTENSION ACTIVITY

ONLINE REGISTRATION

If you are teaching *Internet English* in a traditional classroom, you may want to help students practice filling in registration forms before they go away to set up an E-mail account on their own.

1. Photocopy the registration form on page 19 of the **Teacher's Book.** Make one copy per student. Explain the registration form and then ask students to fill it in using a pen or pencil.

2. Walk around the classroom and encourage students to ask you if they have any problems.

3. After students complete the registration form, tell them to compare their form with a classmate's.

WEB TIP

Ask students to use their name (first name.family name) as their username and a password they can remember easily, (e.g., the name of their hometown). For security reasons, ask students to use their school address instead of their home address and refrain from giving away their telephone number, credit card number, or other important personal information.

NOW STUDENTS WILL USE THEIR COMPUTER AND START SEARCHING THE WEB.

Ask students to open their browser and go to their favorite search engine, type their keywords and then search the Web.

B

Ask students to browse through the results and choose a website that offers free E-mail accounts. Tell students to avoid websites that charge a fee for keeping E-mail accounts.

C

Ask students to write down the name and URL of the website they chose.

D

Ask students to fill in the registration form.

E

When students have finished setting up their E-mail account, ask them to write down their full E-mail address and password in their book.

VOCABULARY LOG

Make a copy of the *Vocabulary Log* (page 98 of the **Teacher's Book**) for each student. Ask students to select five unfamiliar words and phrases from the websites they explored and write them down in their *Vocabulary Log*. For each phrase students should provide its meaning and an example of use.

PAGE 12

Ask students to have a look at the example E-mail format (a Hotmail Compose screen). Explain the different parts of the screen. These are particular to Hotmail, but other E-mail programs have similar functions. For example:

To: This is the line where the sender writes the E-mail address of the primary recipient.

Subject: This is the line where the sender writes what the message is about.

cc: If the sender wants to send a copy of this message to another person (other than the recipient), then he/she writes the E-mail address of this person on the cc: line.

bcc: An address written here (the blind copy line) receives a copy of the message without the knowledge of the primary recipient.

Attachment: Clicking here will allow the sender to select a file or files to be sent along with the E-mail message.

Message: In this section the sender types the message.

QuickList: Clicking here will retrieve a list of nicknames for E-mail addresses that the user has input earlier.

Save Draft: Clicking here allows you to save an unfinished message to complete later.

Now ask students to match each E-mail term with the correct definition. When the students have finished writing, ask them to compare their answers with their partner.

> **ANSWERS**
>
> 1. Message   5. bcc: 9. Cancel
> 2. Send   6. Attachments   10. Spell Check
> 3. Subject: 7. To:
> 4. cc: 8. Save Draft

OPTIONAL

If you have time you can check students' answers in class. For example, ask students:

- *What do you write after* **To:***?*
- *Where do you click to cancel your message?*

NETIQUETTE AND EMOTICONS

1. Photocopy the *Extension Activity* on page 20 of the **Teacher's Book.** Make one copy for each student.

2. Explain the Netiquette rules and ask students to observe these rules whenever they send E-mail messages to people.

3. Explain to students the purpose of emoticons and how to make an emoticon (using a colon, a dash, a parenthesis, a square bracket, etc.), and then show them the list of emoticons. Ask students to tilt the page 90 degrees to the right in order to view the emoticons.

4. Ask students to have a look at the E-mail message and then correct it according to the netiquette rules. Tell students to add an emoticon to the message in the blank.

> **ANSWERS**
>
> **Subject–** There is no subject written on the subject line.
>
> **HI MARIA, WHERE HAVE YOU BEEN?–** This should not be in all capital letters.
>
> **You are a terrible person!–** This is not very nice and could be considered rude.
>
> **Bye–** The sender should always sign his/her name at the end of the message.
>
> **Emoticon–** :-(or :-{

PAGE 13

PREPARATION: Tell students that they will use E-mail in order to introduce themselves to some of their classmates.

Ask students to go around the classroom and ask five or six students for their name and E-mail address. Tell students to use the model dialog for guidance. Ask students to write down their classmates' names and E-mail addresses. If there are any students who did not create an E-mail account, ask them to follow the procedure on page 11 and create an E-mail account.

When students finish writing down their classmates' names and E-mail addresses, ask them to type the E-mail addresses in the address book of their E-mail account and name the group "Group List."

Now ask students to send a message to the "Group List." On the Subject line they should write "My Introduction." In the body of the message they should write a short introduction about themselves, as in the example in the book. After they finish writing their introduction, they should send the message.

Now ask students to read the E-mail messages they received from their classmates, and then answer the question in their book.

OPTIONAL

If you have time you can ask students to share their answers with a partner, in groups or with the rest of the class.

E-MAIL ACTIVITY

PAGE 57

PREPARATION: Tell students that they will use E-mail in order to find information about some of their classmates. Have students work in groups of three or four. Ask students to find out the E-mail addresses of their group's members.

A. Then ask students to write down three questions they would like to ask their group members. Direct their attention to the example questions in the book.

B. Now ask students to send an E-mail message to their group with their questions. Tell them to follow the format in the example (i.e., after each question they should leave an empty line for the answer). On the Subject line they should write "Questions."

C. Now ask students to reply to the E-mail messages they received from their classmates. They should include the original E-mail message in their reply and type their answers in the blank spaces after each question.

D. Ask students to have a look at the replies they received from their classmates and then write down some interesting things about their classmates.

E. Finally, ask students to share the interesting things they learned with a classmate.

IN THE TRADITIONAL CLASSROOM

If you are teaching *Internet English* in a classroom without computers, you can ask students to do the E-mail activity in class without using computers.

1. Put students in groups of three or four. Make copies of the blank E-mail messages on page 21 of the **Teachers' Book.** Give two or three blank E-mail messages to each student (two each for groups of three, three each for groups of four).

2. Ask students to fill in the header of the E-mail messages (To:, Subject:) with a pencil, and then write their three questions in the body of the message following the example format in their book. They need to make one copy for each member of their group.

3. When the students have finished their E-mail messages, ask them to deliver them to their group members.

4. Ask students to read the E-mail messages they received.

5. Tell students to write their answers to the questions, change the information on the header, and return the message to the "sender."

6. Tell students to read their classmates' answers to their questions and then write down some interesting things that they learned about their classmates in **D** on page 57 of the **Student Book.**

7. Finally ask students to share with a classmate interesting things they learned about their group.

Electronic Mail
Extension Activity

ONLINE REGISTRATION

A   This is a typical online registration form. Fill in the form as completely as you can.

Account Information

Username	_____	*(Type your name or a nickname here.)*
Password	_____	*(Choose a word only you know.)*
Verify Password	_____	*(Write your password again here.)*

Information About Yourself

First Name   _____

Family Name   _____

Street Address   _____

_____

City   _____

Zip/Postal Code   _____

Country   _____

Gender   ◯ Male   ◯ Female

Date of Birth   _____

Marital Status   ◯ Single   ◯ Married   ◯ Divorced

Occupation   _____

More About You

Check your favorite hobbies:

◯ Computer Games   ◯ Music   ◯ Food/Cooking   ◯ Movies

◯ Travel   ◯ Cars   ◯ Other: _____

Check your favorite sports:

◯ Baseball   ◯ Soccer   ◯ Basketball   ◯ Golf   ◯ Cycling

◯ Swimming   ◯ Tennis   ◯ Snow Sports   ◯ Other: _____

B   Compare your form with a classmate's. How many things do you have in common?

NETIQUETTE AND EMOTICONS

A Netiquette

There are certain rules of etiquette that people have to follow when using E-mail. Here are some:

• Be nice. Don't send rude messages.

• Always include the subject of your message on the **Subject** line.

• Don't type your message in ALL CAPITAL LETTERS. Typing your message in CAPITAL letters means that you are SHOUTING.

• Always add your name at the end of your message.

B Emoticons

Emoticons are small icons that show emotions. The most common emoticon is the smiley face :-). Here are some more emoticons you can use with your E-mail messages:

:-] a big smile	:-D laughter	;-) a wink
:-(a frown	:-{ really sad	[ ] hugs

C Have a look at the following E-mail message. Correct the mistakes according to the Netiquette rules and write an emoticon in the blank.

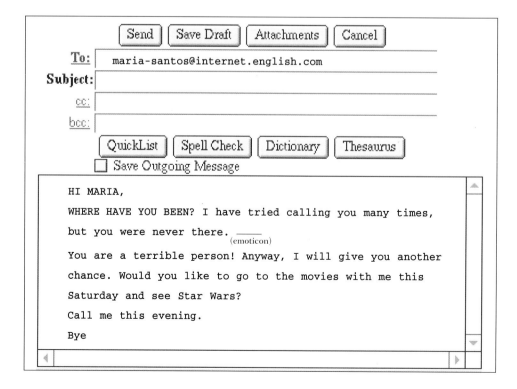

HI MARIA,

WHERE HAVE YOU BEEN? I have tried calling you many times, but you were never there. _____
(emoticon)

You are a terrible person! Anyway, I will give you another chance. Would you like to go to the movies with me this Saturday and see Star Wars?

Call me this evening.

Bye

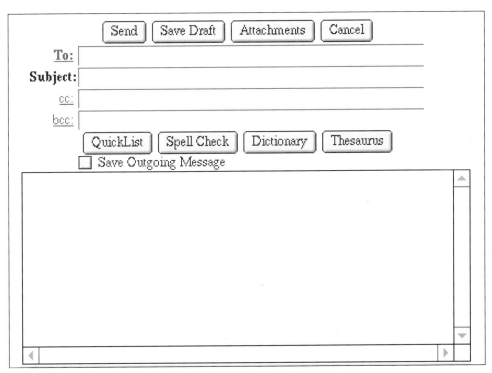

UNIT 3 Electronic Mail
E-Mail Activity

E-MAIL BLANKS

**For use with Student Book, page 57,
in a traditional classroom.**

| Send | Save Draft | Attachments | Cancel |

To:
Subject:
cc:
bcc:

| QuickList | Spell Check | Dictionary | Thesaurus |

☐ Save Outgoing Message

| Send | Save Draft | Attachments | Cancel |

To:
Subject:
cc:
bcc:

| QuickList | Spell Check | Dictionary | Thesaurus |

☐ Save Outgoing Message

Go To: `file:///www`

FREE WEB-BASED E-MAIL ACCOUNTS

1. **RocketMail:** http://www.rocketmail.com/

2. **HotMail:** http://www.hotmail.com/

3. **MailCity:** http://www.mailcity.lycos.com/

4. **Student Center:** http://studentcenter.infomall.org/free-email.html

5. **CNN:** http://www.ccnmail.com/

6. **E-mail.com:** http://www2.email.com/login/login.jhtml

7. **iName:** http://www.iname.com/member/login.page

8. **Excite:** http://www.excite.com/Info/mailexcite/welcome.html

9. **E-Mail Terminology:** http:// www.newbie-u.com/email/terms.html

10. **All About E-Mail (TM): E-mail glossary:** http://www.allaboutemail.com/glossary.html

11. **WhoWhere?** Directories of E-mail addresses, phone numbers, and postal addresses.
    http://www.whowhere.lycos.com/

KEYPAL ORGANIZATIONS

12. **Keypals Club:** The safest way to connect classroom to classroom...student to student...worldwide.
    http://www.mightymedia.com/keypals/

13. **Surf-E-Mates:** A moderated safe list for obtaining keypals.
    http://www.ozkidz.gil.com.au/rm/student/surfe.htm

Add your favorite websites for this unit here:

1. _____

2. _____

3. _____

4. _____

5. _____

UNIT 4 Famous People

IDENTIFY STUDENT BOOK, page 14	Think of famous people for different occupations Ask classmates about famous people they know
PREPARE YOUR SEARCH STUDENT BOOK, page 15	Narrow the search to one famous person Talk about your favorite famous person
SEARCH THE WEB STUDENT BOOK, page 16	Search for biographical information about the famous person
WEB TALK STUDENT BOOK, page 17	Interview two classmates about famous people
PRACTICE PAGE STUDENT BOOK, page 58	Language Window—Talking about past events Computer Project—Create a famous person profile

KEY VOCABULARY

actor/actress	funny	place of birth
athlete	great	politician
beautiful	handsome	profile
career history	important	singer
cool	intelligent	skillful
comedian	knowledgeable	talented
film director	occupation	wonderful

INTRODUCTION

1. Introduce the topic to students. Tell them that this unit is about famous people, i.e. people who are well-known all over the world. Invite students to name some famous people in their country. Ask students what these people are famous for (e.g., famous singer, comedian, actor). If you have time, write some of the names and occupations that students provide you with on the board.

2. Now ask students to open their books. Outline the sequence of activities. Tell students they will think about famous people and choose their favorite one. Then they will find information about their favorite famous person on the Web and share their information with their classmates.

WEB PAGE WARM-UP

PAGE 14

1. Ask students if they can recognize the person in the art (Celine Dion). Students may have difficulty pronouncing her name, so it is a good idea to practice saying it with students.

2. Ask other questions related to the art. For example, ask:

   • *What is this person famous for?*

   • *Can you name any of her songs?*

   • *Do you like her songs?*

   • *What kind of information do you think you could find on this website?*

   • *Have you ever visited a famous person's website?*

PAGE 14

1. Review the vocabulary in the Occupations list and ask students to write the name of at least one famous person for each occupation (at least one of the famous people in each occupation should be from an English-speaking country or internationally famous).

2. At this point, you may want to walk around the classroom offering help, as many students may be having difficulty with the spelling of some of the English-language names.

PAIR WORK: When students have finished their writing task, ask them to compare their answers with a classmate's using the model dialog for guidance.

OPTIONAL

Take some time to ask students about some of the famous people they wrote. For example, ask students:

- *Can you name a famous actor or actress?*
- *Can you name a famous athlete?*
- *Can you name a famous comedian?*

Invite a couple of students to answer each of your questions. If possible write some of the names on the board. In this way students will be exposed to a large number of famous people, widening their repertoire and getting some ideas for the next sections of the unit.

PREPARE YOUR SEARCH

PAGE 15

Ask students to complete the chart by writing the names of their three favorite famous people and their occupations. It is a good idea to walk around the class while students are working in case they need help with spelling unfamiliar names. Encourage students to ask if they are unsure about how to spell certain names.

Now ask students to choose one of their famous people that they would like to research and write

this person's name and occupation in the box provided. Ask students to make sure the person they choose is from an English-speaking country or internationally famous to ensure that they will find English-language websites about this person.

WEB TIP

Walk around the classroom and have a look at students' choices. It is important that the person they have chosen is famous enough to ensure that there will be enough information on the Web about this person. It is all right if students choose a deceased famous person, provided the person is famous enough. Note that students need to use the past tense when talking about deceased famous people as in the model dialog about Princess Diana in **C**.

Ask students to discuss their choice with a classmate using the model dialog provided as a guide. Introduce the vocabulary in the word box and explain any unfamiliar vocabulary. You can also invite students to think of some more words.

OPTIONAL

You may also want to give students some more ways of expressing opinions and preferences. For example:

- *I think that…*
- *In my opinion…*
- *I like…the best*

LANGUAGE WINDOW

At this point it is a good idea to introduce the *Language Window* to students (see page 58 of the **Student Book** and page 26 of the **Teacher's Book**).

EXTENSION ACTIVITY

FAMOUS PEOPLE GAME

1. Photocopy the *Extension Activity* on page 27 of the **Teacher's Book.** Make one copy for each student.

2. Ask students to work in groups of three or four. For each section students should write as many famous people as they can in one minute. After that they should compare their

list with the other group members' and cross out any names that appear on more than one list. The student with the most names remaining is the winner. Ask students to explain any names that the other group members do not know.

SEARCH THE WEB

PAGE 16

1. Now that each student has decided who is his/her favorite famous person, it is time for the Web search. Before writing the keywords they will use for the Web search, students should have a look at the example provided in the book (*Celine Dion biography*). Ask students to write their keywords in the box and make sure they have spelled the name correctly.

> **WEB TIP**
>
> Using the name of the famous person as keywords should be enough for a successful Web search. However, if the famous person has a common name (e.g., *Paul Smith),* then advise students to include the occupation of the famous person along with the name (e.g., *Paul Smith designer).*

2. PREPARATION: Review the chart in part **D** and explain any unfamiliar vocabulary so that students will have a good idea of what they are looking for in a website. Tell students that, when they do the Web search, they have to look for specific information in order to complete the chart. Explain that under Family Information students need to find out if the famous person is married or not, if he/she has any brothers and sisters, etc. Explain that under Interesting Information students should write at least one piece of interesting information about their famous person (e.g., how many languages this famous person can speak, any special events that happened in this person's life).

 NOW STUDENTS WILL USE THEIR COMPUTER AND START SEARCHING THE WEB.

3. Ask students to open their browser, go to their favorite search engine, type the keywords carefully, and then search the Web.

When students get their first page of results ask them to scan the results looking for websites that are "official". Ask students to explore the contents of the selected sites.

After students have explored the websites, ask them to write the name and URL of the one that provides the most interesting information.

Ask students to use information from the website in order to complete the chart about the famous person.

> **VOCABULARY LOG**
>
> Make a copy of the *Vocabulary Log* (page 98 of the **Teacher's Book**) for each student. Ask students to select five unfamiliar words and phrases from the websites they explored and write them down in their *Vocabulary Log*. For each phrase students should provide its meaning and an example of use.

WEB TALK

PAGE 17

1. PREPARATION: Tell students that they will interview two of their classmates about their favorite famous person. Review the sample questions and answers that students can use as a guide for their interviews. Ask students to write their classmates' answers in the charts provided. Remind students that this is a conversation activity (i.e., they are not to simply copy each other's notes).

2. Ask students to go around the classroom and interview two classmates separately. Interviewees should consult their chart on page 16 of the **Student Book.** If there are any students who missed the *Search the Web* session and have not completed the chart on page 16, they can interview their classmates, but they cannot be interviewed.

When students finish their interviews, ask them to look at their classmates' answers in the chart and decide which of the famous people they would like to meet and why. Ask them to write their answers in their book.

OPTIONAL

If you have time, you can ask students to share their answers with their partner, in groups or with the rest of the class.

LANGUAGE WINDOW

PAGE 58

A. Review the different expressions in the *Language Window*. Main points:
- Simple Past Tense
- Regular (**-ed**) / Irregular verbs
- Past Time Expressions (**when** I was…; **yesterday; in** 1993; **last** year/month/week; ten years **ago**)

B. Ask students to write their own examples about past events in their life. This can also be given as homework if there is not enough time during the lesson. Review students' answers and/or ask them to check their answers with their partner.

COMPUTER PROJECT

PAGE 58

1. Project: Ask students to create a profile of their favorite famous person using their word processor. Show them the sample profile in the book. Ask students to:
   - *Open the Web browser*
   - *Go to the website they wrote down during the Search the Web section (page 16).*
   - *Copy images and text to use in the profile from the website to a word-processing document.*

WEB TIP

Refer students to the *Technical Tips* on page 68 of the **Student Book** regarding copying images and text from the Web to a word-processing document. Quickly run through the instructions on how to copy pictures and text from the Web.

---

2. Remind students to list the URL of the website they used to get the information for their famous person profile.

3. Ask students to edit the information they copied, add their own opinions and ideas, arrange the picture(s) and text (see *How to Arrange*

Pictures and Text, page 69), check the spelling, and then save the file as *Yourname.*Famous.

4. If possible ask students to make a printout of their famous person profile.

SHARE YOUR PROJECT

PAGE 58

A. Ask students to E-mail their famous person profile to three or four of their classmates. Ask students to:
- Open their E-mail software.
- Open a **New Message.**
- Type their classmates' E-mail addresses on the **To:** line.
- Type the name of the famous person on the **Subject** line.
- Write a small message such as: *Hi! Have a look at my Famous Person Profile. What do you think?*
- Attach the famous person profile (choose **Attach** or **Attachment** and then choose the profile file in the new window).

B. Ask students to look at their classmates' projects and then answer the questions in their book.

C. Ask students to share their answers with a member of their group.

IN A TRADITIONAL CLASSROOM

If you are teaching *Internet English* in a classroom without computers, you can do the Famous Person Profile in class without using computers.

1. Before the Web Talk, ask students to bring in pictures of their favorite famous person.

2. Each student should also have a blank piece of paper or poster board, colored markers, and a glue stick.

3. Ask students to paste the picture(s) of their favorite famous person on the blank page, and then use the color markers to write some information about the famous person. They can use the information from their chart on page 16 of the **Student Book.**

4. When students have finished their famous person profile, ask them to post their profile in class.

5. Ask students to look at the other students' profiles and answer the questions in **B** of *Share Your Project.*

6. Ask students to share their answers with a classmate.

FAMOUS PEOPLE GAME

Work in groups of three. Start with the *Actors / Actresses* section. Write down the names of as many famous actors and actresses as you can in one minute. Then:

1. Compare your list with your group members'.
2. Cross out any names that appear on more than one list.
3. The student with the most names remaining is the winner.
4. Explain any names that your group members do not know.
5. Repeat with the other categories.

A. Actors / Actresses

_____

_____

_____

B. Singers / Music Groups

_____

_____

_____

C. Athletes

_____

_____

_____

D. Comedians

_____

_____

_____

E. World Leaders / Politicians

_____

_____

_____

Go To: | file:///www|

1. **Xoom.com:** List of links to famous pop and rock artists.
   http://members.xoom.com/exx_info/index.html

2. **Biography.com:** Database of over 20,000 biographies of famous personalities.
   http://www.biography.com/

3. **FamousPeople.com:** Biographical information of a list of famous people.
   http://www.famouspeople.com/famouspeople.html

4. **Famous Actresses Links:** Links to pictures, biography, filmography.
   http:// members.xoom.com/exxy/index.html

5. **Biography Sites:** Over 20,000 short biographies of famous people, both living and dead.
   Biographical dictionary contains more than 25,000 notable men and women who have shaped
   our world from ancient times to the present day.
   http://152.157.38.6/library/biosite.htm

6. **Artistically Correct:** List of some famous artists (painters, sculptors, etc.).
   http://www.netins.net/showcase/myoddwebvice/artpg.html

7. **CelebSites:** The source for celebrity links and information.
   http://www.celebsite.com/

8. **Webfind Movies: Celebrity:** Webfind.net links to celebrities, official sites, fansites.
   http://webfind.net/movies/c/celebrity.html

9. **Lycos Guide to Celebrities**
   http://www-english.lycos.com/entertainment/celebrities/

Add your favorite websites for this unit here:

1. _____

2. _____

3. _____

4. _____

5. _____

UNIT 5 Web Cards

KEY VOCABULARY

address	exciting	preview
animated	future	receive
apartment	graduation	recipient
become	greeting card	screen saver
bon voyage	heritage	sender
bright	occasion	tiny
card message	optional	Valentine's Day
category	personal	wedding
congratulations	personalize	
enter	possible	

INTRODUCTION

1. Introduce the topic to students. Tell them that this unit is about electronic greeting cards (or "Web cards"), i.e., greeting cards that students can send to their friends through the Internet.

2. Now ask students to open their books. Outline the sequence of activities. Tell students they will identify different types of greeting cards, interview their classmates, and decide what kinds of cards to send them. Then they will find websites that allow them to send Web cards for free and send Web cards to their classmates.

Finally they will interview classmates about the cards they received.

WEB PAGE WARM-UP

PAGE 18

Direct students' attention to the Blue Mountain Arts homepage. Ask them if they have ever sent or received an electronic greeting card. For example, ask students:

• *Has anyone ever received a Web card?*

• *Has anyone ever sent a Web card?*

WEB TIP

Explain some of the advantages of electronic greeting cards (e.g., they are environmentally friendly, they are free, they don't have to be mailed in advance, they are delivered instantly, they can have sounds and animation).

IDENTIFY

PAGE 18

1. PREPARATION: Explain to students that there are different types of cards. Ask students what kinds of cards they usually receive (e.g., Christmas cards, New Year's Cards, birthday cards). If possible write the types of cards on the board.

2. Now ask students to read the card messages and match each message with each type of card. You may have to explain some of the vocabulary in the card messages (e.g., "one-derful") and some of the types of cards (e.g., graduation, get well).

PAIR WORK: When students have finished the matching task, ask them to compare their answers with a classmate's using the model dialog for guidance.

OPTIONAL

Take some time to ask students which message goes with which type of card. For example, ask students:

- *"Hoping you'll get better soon"—What kind of card is this message for?*

- *Which message is best for a graduation card?*

PREPARE YOUR SEARCH

PAGE 19

1. PREPARATION: Review the different types of cards and make sure students understand the vocabulary.

2. Ask students to check the types of cards people in their country send to each other. Then ask them to add to the list two more types of cards that are typical in their country.

WEB TIP

Explain to students that sending electronic greeting cards is becoming a widespread custom in English-speaking countries. There are cards for every occasion, and people send cards to each other not only on special celebrations but also on less important occasions (e.g., buying a new house, getting a new job, saying "Thank you" or "Sorry").

1. GROUP WORK: Ask students to form groups of three or four and ask questions to their group members. For each person in their group they have to decide what type of card to send depending on each student's recent experiences or future plans. Tell students that if a member in their group has answered "No" to all the questions, then they can send a "Thank You" card to this group member.

2. Have students write down their group members' names, the types of card they will send, and their E-mail addresses.

LANGUAGE WINDOW

At this point it is a good idea to introduce the *Language Window* to students (see page 59 of the **Student Book** and page 32 of the **Teacher's Book**).

EXTENSION ACTIVITY

SAY IT WITH A CARD!

1. Photocopy the *Extension Activity* on page 33 of the **Teacher's Book.** Make one copy for each student.

2. Read the instructions for **A** and ask students to choose the right card for each occasion. As apology, sympathy, and anniversary cards may be new to students, take a moment to explain those types of cards to them.

ANSWERS

1. d	3. f	5. b	7. c
2. e	4. a	6. g	

3. Read the instructions for **B** and have students complete the matching exercise.

ANSWERS			
1. e	3. d	5. b	7. f
2. a	4. g	6. c	

4. After students have finished **A** and **B,** ask them to compare their answers with a classmate's.

SEARCH THE WEB

PAGE 20

1. PREPARATION: Now that each student has decided what type of card to send each person in his/her group, it is time for the Web search. Tell students that they will look for websites that offer free electronic Web cards and send to their group members. Ask students to use "electronic greeting card" as keywords for their search.

> **WEB TIP**
>
> Explain to students that some websites charge a fee for sending electronic cards. Therefore, students should check that the websites they find offer the service for free, and they should ignore websites that charge a fee.

2. Tell students that when they find a website that allows them to send electronic cards for free, for each card they will send, they will need to fill in a form with specific information. Review the form in **D.** Explain some of the terms used in the form.

 NOW STUDENTS WILL USE THEIR COMPUTER AND START SEARCHING THE WEB.

3. Ask students to open their browser, go to their favorite search engine, type the keywords carefully, and then search the Web.

Ask students to browse through the results and choose the websites that offer free Web cards and have a large collection of cards. Tell students that some sites may offer cards that include sound, music, animation, etc., and there are sites that allow people to design their own card.

Ask students to write down the URL of the website with the best cards.

Ask students to choose the cards they want to send to each member in their group. Then for each card they should complete the form (type their name, E-mail address, the name of the recipient, the E-mail address of the recipient, and their message) and preview the card before sending it.

> **TEACHING TIP**
>
> Make sure that students understand that they need to write their own message in the card.

> **VOCABULARY LOG**
>
> Make a copy of the *Vocabulary Log* (page 98 of the **Teacher's Book**) for each student. Ask students to select five unfamiliar words and phrases from the cards in the website they chose and write them down in their *Vocabulary Log*. For each phrase, students should provide its meaning and an example of use.

WEB TALK

PAGE 21

Ask students to check their E-mail for Web card messages. Each message will explain how to view the Web card. With some Web cards, students need to type a password that will be provided to them in their E-mail message.

After viewing their cards, students should complete the chart. Tell them to write down the types of cards they received and the names of the senders.

Ask students to go around the class and ask their classmates questions to find out what kinds of cards they received. Next to the type of card, students should write the name of the classmate who received such a card.

D

Tell students to report what they found in **C** to a partner.

OPTIONAL

If you have time, you can ask students what types of cards they received. For example, you can ask:

• *Who received a birthday card?*
• *Who received a good luck card?*

LANGUAGE WINDOW

PAGE 59

A. Review the different expressions in the *Language Window*. Explain that such expressions are standard card expressions (i.e., not to be used in spoken English).

B. Ask students to write their wishes for the three different types of cards. This can also be given as homework if there is not enough time during the lesson. Review students' answers and/or ask them to compare their answers with their partner.

COMPUTER PROJECT

PAGE 59

1. PROJECT: Ask students to form groups of three or four and discuss with each group member what type of card to make for him/her (e.g., birthday, congratulations, get well). Then they have to create a card for each member in their group using a picture from Web and their word processor. Show them the sample card in the book. Refer students to the *Technical Tips* (pages 68 of the **Student Book**) regarding how to download pictures and text from the Web to a word processing document.

2. After students copy the picture, they can write their message to their classmate and arrange the picture and text in their document (see *Technical Tips*, page 69).

3. Remind students to list the URL(s) of the website(s) they used to get the information and pictures for their cards.

4. Ask students to save each card in a separate file and save each file as *StudentName*.Card.

5. If possible, ask students to make a printout of their cards.

SHARE YOUR PROJECT

PAGE 59

A. Ask students to E-mail each of their cards to the person they made it for.
   STEPS:
   • Open their E-mail software.
   • Open a **New Message.**
   • Type the classmate's E-mail address on the **To:** line.
   • Type the type of card on the **Subject** line.
   • Write a small message such as: *Hi! Have a look at the card I made for you. What do you think?*
   • Attach the card (choose **Attach** or **Attachment**) and then choose the card file in the new window).

B. Ask students to have a look at the cards they received from their classmates and then answer the questions in their book.

C. Finally ask students to share their answers with their group.

IN A TRADITIONAL CLASSROOM

If you are teaching *Internet English* in a classroom without computers, you can ask students to create their cards in class without using computers.

1. Before the *Web Talk*, ask students to bring the following to class: pictures or cartoons for making cards, a glue stick, color markers, and blank pieces of paper.

2. Ask students to form groups of three or four and then find out some important information for each member in their group. Ask students to create a card for each member in their group. For each card, students should paste or draw pictures on a blank page and then write a message in English.

3. When students have finished their cards, they can give each card to the student they made it for. Alternatively, they can post their cards in class for the recipients to browse through and find.

4. Ask students to look at the cards that their classmates created for them and then answer the questions in **B** of *Share Your Project*.

5. Ask students to share their answers with a member of their group.

Web Cards
Extension Activity

SAY IT WITH A CARD!

A Read the following things that happened to your English-speaking friends (1–7), and choose the right type of card (a–g) to send for each occasion.

Occasions	Types of Cards
1. ☐ Michelle and Simon had a baby girl.	**a.** get well
2. ☐ Phyllis and Alan have been married 50 years.	**b.** bon voyage
3. ☐ You had a fight with Tim.	**c.** happy 21st birthday
4. ☐ Don fell down the stairs and broke his leg.	**d.** new baby
5. ☐ Marion is going to Australia on a diving vacation.	**e.** happy anniversary
6. ☐ Lisa's grandmother died.	**f.** apology
7. ☐ Chris is turning 21 this Monday.	**g.** sympathy

B Below are seven card messages. Match the first half of each message in Column A with the appropriate second half from Column B.

Column A	Column B
1. ☐ Bless your new baby girl.	a. Happy 21st Birthday!
2. ☐ Wishing you another year full of sweet surprises.	b. Thinking of you with deepest sympathy.
3. ☐ Please forgive me.	c. Have a great trip!
4. ☐ Take advantage of this chance to rest.	d. Let's kiss and make up!
5. ☐ May memories keep the one you loved close to you in spirit.	e. May she bring you endless days of sunshine and joy.
6. ☐ A good-bye wave to you on your vacation.	f. Happy Anniversary!
7. ☐ Love and marriage keep getting better every year.	g. Soon you'll be enjoying life in perfect health again.

C After you finish Parts A and B, compare your answers with a classmate's.

Go To: file:///www

1. **Free Electronic/Internet Postcards:** Links to Web sites that offer free electronic/Internet postcards.
   http://www.radix.net/~mschelling/postcard.html

2. **Best Free Electronic Cards:** Large database of links to free electronic cards sites.
   http://www.startingpage.com/html/greeting_cards.htm

3. **Miscellaneous Free Greeting Cards:** Database with links to free electronic card sites.
   http://maxpages.com/oddballs/Free_greeting_cards

4. **Virtual Greeting Cards:** Database with links to electronic cards sites.
   http://www.cardweaver.com/

5. **Free Greeting Cards:** Database with links to electronic cards sites.
   http://members.aol.com/bluuebch/card.html

6. **Blue Mountain Arts:** Free animated cards with sound for every occasion.
   http://www1.bluemountain.com/

7. **E-Cards:** Free electronic cards.
   http://www.e-cards.com/

8. **123 Free Virtual Cyber Greeting Cards:** Guide to over 2000 electronic greeting card sites.
   http://rats2u.com/index.htm/

Add your favorite websites for this unit here:

1. _____
2. _____
3. _____
4. _____
5. _____

UNIT 6 Study Abroad

KEY VOCABULARY

abroad	enroll	sightseeing
academic	experience	social activities
accommodations	fee	student
brochure	firsthand	residence
business	host family	TOEFL
certificate	length	tour
communicate	location	university
country	museum	workshop
culture	preparation	

INTRODUCTION

1. Introduce the topic to students. Tell them that this unit is about studying English abroad in an English-speaking country.

2. Now ask students to open their books. Outline the sequence of activities. Tell students they will think about different reasons for studying abroad; then they will choose a country to study in and an English course; next they will search the Web and find information about a suitable English language program; and finally they will conduct an interview about the program.

PHOTO WARM-UP

PAGE 22

Ask students to have a look at the picture. Ask them questions about it. For example:

- *What are these people doing?*

- *Where are they?*

- *Where do you think they are from?*

- *Would you like to study abroad? Why or why not?*

- *Where would you like to go?*

PAGE 22

A

1. Review the list of reasons for studying abroad and explain any unfamiliar vocabulary. Ask students to check the best reasons for studying abroad.

2. Ask students to list five English-speaking countries where they could study English (e.g., Britain, USA, Canada, Australia, New Zealand).

B

PAIR WORK: When students have finished writing, ask them to compare their answers with a classmate's using the model dialog for guidance.

OPTIONAL

Take some time to ask students aloud in class some of the reasons they would like to study overseas. For example, ask individual students:

- *Who would like to experience a different culture firsthand?*

- *Who would like to make friends from different countries?*

PREPARE YOUR SEARCH

PAGE 23

A

Review the vocabulary in the chart (i.e., types of English courses, social activities, accommodations). Then ask students to add two more items to each list if they can. For example:

- English Courses: English for Academic Purposes (EAP), English Pronunciation, Summer Vacation Course, English Through Computers, General English, TOEIC, TOEFL, IELTS.

- Social Activities: go skiing, go diving, go to the cinema, go to the theater, go to a concert.

- Accommodations: Bed and Breakfast (B&B), hostel, hotel, staying with friends/relatives.

B

Ask students to write their favorite English courses, social activities and accommodations.

C

Ask students to choose a course they would like to research and a location where they would like to study.

TEACHING TIP

Walk around the classroom and have a look at students' choices. Students may need your help with the English spelling of city names (e.g., London, San Francisco, Los Angeles). Encourage students to ask you if they are unsure about the spelling of city names.

D

Ask students to discuss their choice with a classmate using the model dialog provided as a guide.

OPTIONAL

PAIR WORK: Tell students to explain to their partner why they chose the particular course and the particular location. For example, students could take turns asking each other:

- *Why do you want to study Business English?*

- *Why do you want to study in London?*

- *Why do you want to stay with a host family?*

LANGUAGE WINDOW

At this point it is a good idea to introduce the *Language Window* to students (see page 60 of the **Student Book** and page 25 of the **Teacher's Book**).

EXTENSION ACTIVITY

APPLICATION FOR ENROLLMENT

1. Tell students that when they decide to study English abroad they will need to fill in an application form. Copy the *Extension Activity* on page 39 of the **Teacher's Book** and give it to students. Review the form and explain any vocabulary that students do not understand.

2. Ask students to complete the application form with information about themselves.

3. When students have finished writing, ask them to compare their form with a classmate's.

SEARCH THE WEB

PAGE 24

A

1. PREPARATION: Tell students that they will search the Web looking for information on English courses. Ask students to have a look at the example keywords in their book.

2. Ask students to write the keywords for their search. Example keywords:
   - English school *city*
   - ESL course *city*
   - English course *city*
   - *type of course city* (Business English London)

> **TEACHING TIP**
>
> Walk around the classroom and make sure that students have spelled the keywords correctly.

 NOW STUDENTS WILL USE THEIR COMPUTER AND START SEARCHING THE WEB.

3. Ask students to open their browser, go to their favorite search engine, type the keywords carefully, and then search the Web.

> **WEB TIP**
>
> You may want to direct students to databases of English Language Schools for International students. Such databases usually contain lists of ESL schools in different English-speaking countries. A number of databases are included in the list of *Useful URLs* on page 40 of the **Teacher's Book.**

B

Ask students to scan the results, looking for websites that contain the information they need in order to complete the chart on page 24.

1. Ask students to explore the contents of a few websites and then choose one that contains all the information they need.

2. Review the chart on page 24 in advance to show students what they will be looking for in a site. Tell students they will look for specific information about their course in order to complete the chart (e.g., the name of the school, its location, the course name).

> **WEB TIP**
>
> It may be useful to tell students that large academic institutions such as universities have .edu or .ac as part of their URL so that when students scan the search results, they can choose to explore the contents of such websites.

 C

Tell students to write down the name of the school, its location, and the URL of the website they chose.

 D

Ask students to use the information from the website in order to complete the chart.

> **VOCABULARY LOG**
>
> Make a copy of the *Vocabulary Log* (page 97 of the **Teacher's Book**) for each student. Ask students to select five unfamiliar words and phrases from the websites they explored and write them down in their *Vocabulary Log*. For each phrase students should provide its meaning and an example of use.

WEB TALK

PAGE 25

 A

1. PREPARATION: Tell students that they will interview a classmate about the course they chose to study. Review the table with the sample questions and answers that students can use as a guide for their interview. Ask students to write their classmate's answers in the chart provided. Remind students that this is a conversation activity (i.e., they are not to simply copy each other's notes).

2. Ask students to find a partner and carry out the interview. The interviewee should consult his/her chart on page 24 of the **Student Book.** If there are any students who missed the *Search the Web* session and have not completed the chart, they can interview their classmates, but they cannot be interviewed.

When students finish their interviews, ask them to look at their classmate's answers and answer the questions in the book.

LANGUAGE WINDOW

PAGE 60

A. Review the expressions in the *Language Window*. Main points:
- Talking about future plans
- Different degrees of certainty with examples in the *Language Window* arranged from the most certain (going to) to the least certain (might).

B. Ask students to write down their plans for their summer vacation. This can also be given as homework if there is not enough time during the lesson. Review students' answers and/or ask them to compare their answers with a classmate.

COMPUTER PROJECT

PAGE 60

1. PROJECT: Ask students to create a brochure of the school they have chosen using their word processor. Show them the sample brochure in the book. Refer students to the *Technical Tips* (page 68 of the **Student Book**) regarding how to download pictures and text from the Web to a word processing document.

2. Remind students to list the URL(s) of the website(s) they used to get the information and pictures for their brochure.

3. Ask students to edit the information they copied, add their own opinions and ideas, arrange the picture(s) and text in their document (see *Technical Tips*, page 69), check the spelling, and then save the file as *YourName*.School.

4. If possible, ask students to make a printout of their brochure. It may be useful to organize students to take turns when printing their projects to avoid printer jams.

SHARE YOUR PROJECT

PAGE 60

A. In groups of three or four, ask students to E-mail

their brochure to their classmates.

Steps:
- Open their E-mail software.
- Open a **New Message.**
- Type the classmates' E-mail addresses on the **To:** line.
- Type the name of the school and its location on the **Subject** line.
- Write a small message such as: *Hi! Have a look at the school I chose to attend. What do you think?*
- Attach the brochure (choose **Attach** or **Attachment** and then choose the brochure file in the new window).

B. Ask students to have a look at the brochures they received from their classmates and then answer the questions in their book.

C. Finally, ask students to share their answers with a member of their group.

IN A TRADITIONAL CLASSROOM

If you are teaching *Internet English* in a classroom without computers, you can ask students to create their brochure in class without using computers.

1. Before the *Web Talk*, ask students to bring the following to class: pictures related to English language schools from magazines (or pictures they printed from the Web), a glue stick, color markers, and blank pieces of paper or poster board.

2. Ask students to create a brochure for the school they have chosen to attend. Ask them to paste the picture(s) on the blank paper or poster board, and then use the color markers to write some information about the school. They can use the information from their chart on page 24.

3. When students have finished their brochure, they can post it in class.

4. Ask students to have a look at the brochures that their classmates created and then answer the questions in **B** of *Share Your Project*.

5. Ask students to share their answers with a classmate.

APPLICATION FOR ENROLLMENT

A This is an Application for Enrollment for an English school. Complete this form with information about yourself.

Application for Enrollment: School of English

School Registration Information:

first name: _____ family name: _____

date of birth: _____ gender: ☐ male ☐ female

street address: _____

city: _____

postcode: _____ country: _____

telephone: _____ E-mail address: _____

nationality: _____

course chosen: _____

Homestay Application Information:

Do you smoke? ☐ yes ☐ no

Do you prefer a home with pets?   ☐ yes   ☐ no   ☐ don't care

              with children?   ☐ yes   ☐ no   ☐ don't care

Please indicate your favorite activities:

☐ swimming	☐ jogging	☐ movies
☐ tennis	☐ skateboarding	☐ computers
☐ basketball	☐ camping	☐ video games
☐ volleyball	☐ cooking	☐ theatre
☐ golf	☐ shopping	☐ singing
☐ cycling	☐ photography	☐ reading
☐ soccer	☐ travelling	☐ musical instruments
☐ fishing	☐ dancing	☐ other _____
☐ sailing	☐ classical music	
☐ hiking	☐ modern music	

B Now compare your application with a classmate's.

Go To: file:///www

1. **Global Study:** Directory of ESL center websites in Great Britain. Also links to global study directories in the US, Australia, Canada, New Zealand, and Ireland.

    http://www.globalstudy.com/esl/uk/

2. **Europa Pages - The EFL Directory:** A to Z List of English language courses in Britain.

    http://www.europa-pages.co.uk/uk/courses_AZ.html

3. **CET - Canadian Educational Tours:** Agency that offers information about language courses in Canada.

    http://www.cetcanada.com/directory.htm

4. **EI (Education International) Worldwide:** Information and links to English language programs in Australia, New Zealand, Britain, the US, and Canada.

    http://www.eiworldwide.com/default.htm

5. **Knowledge 3000 - ESL Schools and Other Sites:** Links to ESL schools.

    http://toefl.telecampus.com/schools.html

6. **EnglishCLUB.net :** Links to ESL schools around the world.

    http://www.englishclub.net/links/efl_schools.htm

7. **Study in the USA:** A resource for international students.

    http://www.studyusa.com/

8. **Aichi Institute of Technology:** Links to ESL schools around the world.

    http://www.aitech.ac.jp/~iteslj/links/ESL/Schools/

9. **ESL Net:** Links to ESL schools around the world.

    http://www.esl.net/index.html

10. **Studyesl:** Links to ESL schools and information for Korean students.

    http://www.studyesl.com/about.html

Add your favorite websites for this unit here:

1. _____

2. _____

3. _____

4. _____

5. _____

UNIT 7 Eating Out

KEY VOCABULARY

appetizer	dim sum	lush	starter
authentic	fast food	main course	steak house
bamboo	french fries	meal	stylish
blinds	goat	memorable	T-bone steak
beverage	green curry	menu	tandoori
burgers	Indian	modern	tempura
ceiling fans	international	order	Thai
check	Italian	patio	tropical
Chinese	Japanese	romantic	
delicacy	kimchee	setting	
dessert	Korean	spaghetti carbonara	

INTRODUCTION

1. Introduce the topic to students. Tell them that this unit is about exploring the websites of restaurants around the world.

2. Now ask students to open their books. Outline the sequence of activities. Tell students that first they will identify different types of international foods; then they will choose a type of restaurant to search for on the Web; and finally, they will role-play ordering dinner at a restaurant.

PHOTO WARM-UP

PAGE 26

Ask students to have a look at the picture of different ethnic foods. Ask students questions, for example:

- *Do you like trying different foods from foreign countries?*

- *How often do you go to ethnic restaurants?*

- *What international foods can you make?*

PAGE 26

1. Ask students to look at the picture and write down the food items they can recognize.

ANSWERS

sushi, tandoori chicken, tacos, fish 'n' chips, kiwi fruit, nan, champagne, apple pie, kimchee, gyoza, caviar

2. Now ask students to write down the country of origin for each food item.

ANSWERS

sushi–Japan, tandoori chicken–India, tacos–Mexico, fish 'n' chips–Britain, kiwi fruit–New Zealand, nan–India, champagne–France, apple pie–USA, kimchee–Korea, gyoza–China, caviar–Russia

PAIR WORK: When students have finished writing, ask them to compare their answers with a classmate's using the model dialog for guidance.

OPTIONAL

Take some time to ask students if they have ever tried any of the dishes in the picture or how often they eat these dishes. For example, ask students:

- *Have you ever tried tandoori chicken? Did you like it?*

- *How often do you eat sushi? Every day, twice a week...?*

PAGE 27

Review the types of restaurants in the chart. Then ask students to write a food item from the box or one of their own for each type of restaurant.

POSSIBLE ANSWERS

1. dim sum	5. green curry
2. kimchee	6. tandoori chicken
3. tempura	7. T-bone steak
4. spaghetti carbonara	8. burger and fries

OPTIONAL

After students have completed the chart, ask them to provide you with some of the items they wrote. Share any original answers they found with the class.

Ask students to write down their three favorite types of restaurants and a food item for each restaurant.

Ask students to choose a type of restaurant and a food to eat from their list of favorites.

TEACHING TIP

Walk around the classroom and have a look at students' choices. Make sure that they have spelled the items correctly. Encourage students to ask you if they are unsure about the spelling of certain items.

Ask students to discuss their choices with a classmate using the model dialog as a guide.

LANGUAGE WINDOW

At this point it is a good idea to introduce the *Language Window* to students (see page 61 of the **Student Book** and page 44 of the **Teacher's Book**).

EXTENSION ACTIVITY

WHAT'S FOR DINNER?

1. Photocopy the *Extension Activity* on page 45 of the **Teacher's Book.** Make one copy for each student.

2. Ask students to practice the conversation with

a classmate. After they finish, ask them to change roles and practice the conversation again.

3. Ask students to complete the chart (type of food, type of restaurant, location).

4. Now ask students to practice the conversation with three different classmates. Each time they practice they should substitute a different type of food, type of restaurant, and location from the chart.

SEARCH THE WEB

PAGE 28

1. Now that each student has decided what type of restaurant they like, it is time for the Web search. Tell students that they will look for a restaurant around the world, and then they will use the menu information to complete the chart in **D**. Ask students to use the type of restaurant they chose and *menu* as keywords for their search. Show them the example provided in the book and ask students to write their keywords in the box.

2. Tell students that they will explore the websites of restaurants around the world, choose their favorite one, and write down the name, its location and URL. Then they will have a look at the restaurant menu and fill in the chart. Review the chart with the students and explain any unfamiliar vocabulary (e.g., appetizers, starters, beverages).

NOW STUDENTS WILL USE THEIR COMPUTER AND START SEARCHING THE WEB.

3. Ask students to open their browser and go to their favorite search engine, type their keywords, and then search the Web.

Ask students to browse through the results and choose the websites that offer information about restaurants and menus.

WEB TIP

If your students have a hard time finding a restaurant, you can direct them to the restaurant databases on page 46 of the **Teacher's Book.**

Ask students to choose a restaurant website with a menu and write down the restaurant name, the city and country it is located in, and the URL of the website.

Ask students to choose what they would like to order and write the menu items in the chart provided.

Ask students to print out the menu. If printing is impossible, students should copy part or all of the menu by hand to use in the role-play activity in the *Web Talk* on page 29 of the **Student Book.**

VOCABULARY LOG

Make a copy of the *Vocabulary Log* (page 98 of the **Teacher's Book**) for each student. Ask students to select five unfamiliar words and phrases from the websites they explored and write them down in their *Vocabulary Log*. For each phrase students should provide its meaning and an example of use.

WEB TALK

PAGE 29

1. PREPARATION: Tell students that they will role-play ordering dinner at a restaurant. Have students form pairs. One student plays the customer and the other plays the waiter. Before starting, the customer should give to the waiter the menu he/she found on the Web.

2. Review the sample questions and answers that students can use as a guide for their role-play. Ask students to write their classmate's order in the check provided.

After students have finished their role-play they can change roles and repeat it. If there are any students who missed the *Search the Web* session and don't have menu information, they can play the waiter, but they cannot play the customer.

OPTIONAL

If you have time you can ask students to share some of the restaurant and menu information they found on the Web with a partner or in groups.

LANGUAGE WINDOW

PAGE 61

A. Review the expressions in the *Language Window*. Main points:
- Making requests
- Degrees of politeness

B. Ask students to write five requests of their own. This can also be given as homework if there is not enough time during the lesson. Review students' answers and/or ask them to compare their answers with a classmate's.

COMPUTER PROJECT

PAGE 61

1. PROJECT: Ask students to create a restaurant brochure using their word processor. Show them the sample brochure in the book. Refer students to the *Technical Tips* (page 68 of the **Student Book**) regarding how to download pictures and text from the Web to a word processing document.

2. Remind students to list the URL(s) of the website(s) they used to get the pictures and information about their restaurant brochure.

3. Ask students to edit the information they copied, add their own ideas, arrange the pictures and text in their document (see *Technical Tips*, page 69), check the spelling, and then save the file as *YourName*.Food.

4. If possible ask students to make a printout of their restaurant brochure. It maybe useful to organize students to take turns when printing their projects to avoid printer jams.

SHARE YOUR PROJECT

PAGE 61

A. Ask students to E-mail their restaurant brochure to three or four of their classmates.

Steps:
- Open their E-mail software.
- Open a **New Message.**
- Type the classmates' E-mail addresses on the **To:** line.
- Type the name of the restaurant on the **Subject** line.
- Write a small message such as: *Hi! Have a look at my restaurant brochure. What do you think?*
- Attach the restaurant brochure (choose **Attach** or **Attachment** and then choose the brochure file in the new window).

B. Ask students to have a look at the restaurant brochures they received from their classmates and then answer the questions in their book.

C. Finally ask students to share their answers with a member of their group.

IN A TRADITIONAL CLASSROOM

If you are teaching *Internet English* in a classroom without computers, you can ask students to create their restaurant brochure in class without using computers.

1. Before the *Web Talk*, ask students to bring the following to class: pictures of restaurants from magazines (or pictures they printed from the Web), a glue stick, color markers, and blank pieces of paper or poster board.

2. Ask students to create a restaurant brochure. Ask them to paste the picture(s) on the blank paper or poster board, and then use the color markers to write some information about the restaurant. They can use the restaurant and menu information from *Search the Web* (page 28 of the **Student Book**).

3. When students have finished their restaurant brochure, they can post it in class.

4. Ask students to have a look at the restaurant brochures that their classmates created and then answer the questions in **B** of *Share Your Project*.

5. Finally ask students to share their answers with a member of their group.

WHAT'S FOR DINNER?

A Practice this conversation with a classmate. Then change roles and practice again.

> **A:** I'm too tired to cook tonight.
>
> **B:** Would you like to go to a restaurant?
>
> **A:** That's a good idea.
>
> **B:** Well, how about some **pizza** at the **Italian** restaurant **downtown**?
>
> **A:** Hmm. I don't feel like eating **pizza** tonight.
>
> **B:** OK. What do you feel like?
>
> **A:** **Pork fried rice**.
>
> **B:** Sounds good. Where shall we go?
>
> **A:** There is a good **Chinese** restaurant **near the park**.
>
> **B:** What time shall we go?
>
> **A:** I'll make a reservation for 7:30.

B Now think of three types of food that you would like eat. Then write a type of restaurant and a location for each one in the chart below.

Type of Food	Type of Restaurant	Location
pizza	Italian	downtown
pork fried rice	Chinese	near the park
1a.	1b.	1c.
2a.	2b.	2c.
3a.	3b.	3c.

C Now practice the conversation with three different classmates. Each time, use a different type of food, type of restaurant, and location from the chart.

Go To: file:///www

1. **Dining Databases Search Engines:** Thousands of directly accessible search engines are available at the Internet's database of databases.

    http://www.internets.com/sdining.htm

2. **MenuWeb:** Restaurant menus database.

    http:// www.menuweb.com/menuweb.htm

3. **The Sushi World Guide:** A guide to Japanese restaurants outside Japan.

    http://www.sushi.infogate.de/

4. **The ULTIMATE Restaurant Directory:** A list of restaurant guides.

    http://www.orbweavers.com/ULTIMATE/listallguides.asp

5. **FoodWeb:** A collection of international restaurant guides by country.

    http://www.foodweb.com/w.w.bites/internationallrestguides.html

6. **Travelfacts Restaurant Search**

    http://www.travelfacts.com/tfacts/htm/searchrest.htm

7. **DineSite:** Nationwide dining guide and restaurant search with restaurant reviews, descriptions, pictures, menus, and links—guide to over 19,000 US cities.

    http://www.dinesite.com/

You can also access restaurant guides for specific cities. For example:

8. **The Restaurant Guide:** New York's largest online dining database.

    http://www.the-restaurant-guide.com/

9. **Bostondine.com:** A searchable database listing restaurants in Boston.

    http://www.bostondine.com/

Add your favorite websites for this unit here:

1. _____
2. _____
3. _____
4. _____
5. _____

UNIT 8   Shopping Spree

IDENTIFY **STUDENT BOOK,** page 30	Ways to shop Things to buy
PREPARE YOUR SEARCH **STUDENT BOOK,** page 31	Think of things to buy online Choose three items to buy online
SEARCH THE WEB **STUDENT BOOK,** page 32	Look for online shopping websites Collect information about specific items
WEB TALK **STUDENT BOOK,** page 33	Interview three classmates about their shopping experience
PRACTICE PAGE **STUDENT BOOK,** page 62	Language Window—Asking for and saying prices Computer Project—Create a shopping catalog

KEY VOCABULARY

accessories	door-to-door	low waist	soccer ball
alarm clock	equipment	mail order	skis
catalog	fitness	narrow fit	snowboard
cell phone	fly	online	sunglasses
cents	heavyweight	payment	straight leg
cotton	hundred	price	tank
credit card	in-line skates	salesperson	waist
description	jeans	shopping spree	watch
dollar(s)	leg	size	zip fly

INTRODUCTION

1. Begin with questions about shopping. For example, ask students:

   • *Who likes shopping?*

   • *How often do you go shopping?*

2. Introduce the topic to students. Tell them that this unit is about online shopping, i.e., shopping on the Internet.

3. Now ask students to open their books. Outline the sequence of activities. Tell students that first they will talk about different ways of shopping, then choose three things to buy on the Internet; after that they will search for online shopping websites and collect information about the things they chose to buy; finally, they will share information about their shopping experience with their classmates.

WEB PAGE WARM-UP

PAGE 30

1. Ask students to have a look at the picture of the J.Crew online shopping website. Ask students:

   • *Do you know J.Crew?*

   • *Do you like J.Crew products?*

   • *What other companies do you know that have online shopping websites?*

2. Explain some of the advantages of online shopping (e.g., wider variety, cheaper prices, it's easy). Also talk about the disadvantages of online shopping (e.g., you can't try out what you buy, you can only see a picture of the item, shipping can be costly, delivery can take time).

IDENTIFY

PAGE 30

1. Review the different ways of shopping listed in the book. Make sure students understand the differences.

2. Ask students to write down at least two things that they would buy (or even things that they have bought in the past) using each of the different ways of shopping.

PAIR WORK: When students have finished writing, ask them to compare their answers with a classmate using the model dialog for guidance.

OPTIONAL

Take some time to ask students what they would buy using each of the different ways of shopping. For example, ask students:

• *What would you buy from a mail-order catalog?*

• *What would you buy at a store?*

PREPARE YOUR SEARCH

PAGE 31

1. Review the vocabulary items in the chart (Clothes and Accessories, Sports and Fitness Equipment, Electronic Equipment).

2. Ask students to write three more items in each column. For example:

• *Clothes and Accessories:* shoes, bag, jacket, skirt, baseball cap, jewelry.

• *Sports and Fitness Equipment:* fishing rod, running shoes, tennis racquet, baseball mitt, camping equipment, golf clubs.

• *Electronic Equipment:* CD player, DVD player, walkman, stereo, laser printer, modem, fax machine, electronic dictionary.

OPTIONAL

After students have completed the table, ask them to provide you with some of the items they wrote. If you have time, write some of the items on the board. For example, ask students:

• *What are some clothes and accessories that you wrote?*

• *What are some items of sports and fitness equipment that you wrote?*

Now ask students to choose three things to buy online and the price they would like to pay for each thing. They may write the prices in their country's currency or in US dollars which is a currency many websites use.

Ask students to discuss their choices with a classmate using the model dialog as a guide.

LANGUAGE WINDOW

At this point it is a good idea to introduce the *Language Window* to students (see page 62 of the **Student Book** and page 49 of the **Teacher's Book**).

EXTENSION ACTIVITY

GOING SHOPPING

1. Photocopy the *Extension Activity* on page 51 of the **Teacher's Book.** Make one copy for each student.

2. Ask students to practice the conversation with a classmate. After they finish, ask them to change roles and practice the conversation again.

3. Review the vocabulary in the chart. Ask students to add one more word in each column. For method of payment they can re-use one of the given examples.

4. Ask students to practice the conversation with three different classmates. Each time ask students to use a different item, size, feature, price, and method of payment from the chart.

SEARCH THE WEB

PAGE 32

1. Now that each student has decided what to buy from the Internet, it is time for the Web search. Tell them that they can use shopping and the name of an item as keywords for their search. They will need to do three searches, one for each item they want to buy. Ask them to look at the example keywords in the book, and then write the keywords for their searches or browse through the shopping links listed in their favorite Web directory.

 NOW STUDENTS WILL USE THEIR COMPUTER AND START SEARCHING THE WEB.

2. Ask students to open their browser and go to their favorite search engine, type in their keywords and then search the Web.

> **WEB TIP**
>
> Remind students that this is a "virtual" shopping spree, and students should not actually order anything, complete and/or submit any online order forms, or give out any credit card information. Alert them to the fact that some sites are not secure enough for credit cards. Advise students to always choose a secure website for credit card purchases.

Ask students to browse through the results and choose the websites that offer the things they want to buy as well as the prices.

Ask students to write down the item, company name, and URL for each of the three websites.

> **VOCABULARY LOG**
>
> Make a copy of the *Vocabulary Log* (page 98 of the **Teacher's Book**) for each student. Ask students to select five unfamiliar words and phrases from the websites they explored and write them down in their *Vocabulary Log*. For each phrase students should provide its meaning and an example of its use.

WEB TALK

PAGE 33

1. PREPARATION: Inform students that they will interview three of their classmates about their shopping spree. Review the sample questions and answers that students can use as a guide for their interviews. Ask students to write their classmates' answers in the charts provided.

2. Ask students to find one classmate at a time and carry out the interview. The interviewee should consult his/her chart on page 32. If there are any students who missed the *Search the Web* session and have not completed the chart on page 32, they can interview their classmates, but they cannot be interviewed.

When students finish their interviews, ask them to look at their classmates' answers and write who spent the most money.

LANGUAGE WINDOW

PAGE 62

A. Review the expressions in the *Language Window*. Main points:

• Different ways of saying the prices.

• Dollar decimal system.

B. Ask students to write the prices in full and then practice saying them. This can also be given as homework if there is not enough time during the lesson. Review students' answers and/or ask them to compare their answers with a classmate's.

COMPUTER PROJECT

PAGE 62

1. PROJECT: Ask students to create one page of an online shopping catalog using their word processor. Show them the sample catalog page in the book. Refer students to the *Technical Tips* (page 68 of the **Student Book**) regarding how to download pictures and text from the Web to a word processing document.

2. Remind students to list the URLs of all the websites they used to get the pictures and information about the items on their catalog page.

3. Ask students to edit the information they copied, arrange the pictures and text in their document (see *Technical Tips*, page 69), think of a name for their online shop, check the spelling, and then save the file as *YourName*.Shop.

4. If possible ask students to make a printout of their catalog. It may be useful to organize students to take turns when printing their projects to avoid printing jams.

SHARE YOUR PROJECT

PAGE 62

A. Ask students to E-mail their catalog to three or four of their classmates.

Steps:

- Open their E-mail software.
- Open a **New Message.**
- Type their classmates' E-mail addresses on the **To:** line.
- Type the name of the online shop on the **Subject** line.

- Write a small message such as: *Hi! Have a look at my online shopping catalog. Would you like to order something from it?*
- Attach the catalog (choose **Attach** or **Attachment** and then choose the catalog file in the new window).

B. Ask students to have a look at the shopping catalogs they received from their classmates and then choose one thing to buy from each catalog. Ask students to send an E-mail to each member in their group and order the item they want to buy from each member's catalog.

After students finish their orders, they should answer the questions in their book.

C. Finally ask students to share their answers with a member of their group.

IN THE TRADITIONAL CLASSROOM

If you are teaching *Internet English* in a classroom without computers, you can ask students to create their catalog in class without using computers.

1. Before the *Web Talk*, ask students to bring the following to class: pictures of clothes and accessories, sports and fitness equipment, and electronic equipment from magazines (or pictures they printed from the Web), a glue stick, color markers, and blank pieces of paper or poster board.

2. Ask students to create a shopping catalog page. Ask them to paste the pictures on a blank sheet of paper or poster board, and then use the color markers to write some information about each of the items in the catalog. They can use the information from their chart on page 32.

3. When students have finished their catalog, ask students to form groups of three or four and share their shopping catalog pages.

4. Ask students to have a look at their group members' catalogs, order one item from each catalog, and then answer the questions in **B** of *Share Your Project*.

5. Finally, ask students to share their answers with a member of their group.

Shopping Spree
Extension Activity

A Practice this conversation with a classmate. Then change roles and practice again.

Clerk:	May I help you?
Customer:	Yes. I am looking for a <u>**baseball cap**</u>.
Clerk:	What size do you want?
Customer:	<u>**Medium**</u>.
Clerk:	Well, how about this one?
Customer:	Can I try on the <u>**blue**</u> one?
Clerk:	Here you are.
Customer:	It looks good. How much is it?
Clerk:	It's <u>**$14.95**</u>.
Customer:	Can I pay <u>**by credit card**</u>?
Clerk:	Sure.

B Review the words in the chart below. Then write one more word in each column.

Item	Size	Feature	Price	Method of Payment
baseball cap	medium	blue	$14.95	by credit card
jacket	large	leather	$390.00	by check
sweater	extra large	striped	$32.80	cash
a.	b.	c.	d.	e.

C Now practice the conversation with three different classmates. Each time, use a different item, size, feature, price, and method of payment from the chart.

Go To: `file:///www.`

1. **Yahoo!:** Directory of online shops.
   http://shopping.yahoo.com/

2. **Lycos:** Links to online shops.
   http://www.lycos.com/shopnet/

3. **Excite:** Links to online shops.
   http://www.excite.com/shopping/

4. **AltaVista:** Links to online shops.
   http://shopping.altavista.com/

5. **Webcrawler:** Links to online shops.
   http://www.webcrawler.com/shopping/

6. **Hotbot:** Directory of links to online shops.
   http://shop.hotbot.com/

7. **The Gap Online Store**
   http://www.gap.com/onlinestore/gap/

8. **L.L. Bean Online**
   http://www.llbean.com/

9. **Marks and Spencer Online**
   http://www.marks-and-spencer.co.uk/

10. **The Body Shop Online**
    http://www.the-body-shop.com/

11. **Designers Direct Online**
    http://www.designersdirect.com/

Add your favorite websites for this unit here:

1. _____
2. _____
3. _____
4. _____
5. _____

UNIT 9   Watching Movies

IDENTIFY STUDENT BOOK, page 34	Movies and movie ratings
PREPARE YOUR SEARCH STUDENT BOOK, page 35	Different types of movies Describing movies Choose a movie to see
SEARCH THE WEB STUDENT BOOK, page 36	Find movie databases Collect information about a movie
WEB TALK STUDENT BOOK, page 37	Interview classmates about their movie choice
PRACTICE PAGE STUDENT BOOK, page 63	Language Window—Expressing opinions about movies Computer Project—Create a movie advertisement

KEY VOCABULARY

Academy Award	computer graphics	newsletter	sad
action movie	courage	oceangoing	scary
actor	database	passenger	science-fiction
actress	director	plot	setting
advertisement	fall in love	popular	special effects
animated movie	film	preview	violent
boring	horror movie	rating	weird
box office hit	inspire	(movie) release	
cash	interesting	romantic	
comedy	love story	sacrifice	

INTRODUCTION

1. Introduce the topic to students. Tell them that this unit is about movies.

2. Now ask students to open their books. Outline the sequence of activities. Tell students that they will rate some movies that they have seen recently, then they will choose a movie that they would like to see, next they will search the Web for movie information, and finally they will talk with their classmates about the movies they chose.

WEB PAGE WARM-UP

Ask students to have a look at the Moviefinder Web page. Ask them some questions about the graphic. For example:

- *How do you usually find out about movies? In a newspaper? On TV?*

- *Do you know any of the actors or movies on this Web page?*

- *Have you ever searched for movie information on the Internet? Would you like to?*

PAGE 34

Introduce the different ratings to students. Then ask students to write down four movies they saw recently and then rate each movie.

> **TEACHING TIP**
>
> Students can write down movies in English or in other languages that they have seen either at the cinema or on video. You may want to walk around the classroom in case students need your help with the spelling of English language movie titles.

PAIR WORK: When students have finished writing, ask them to discuss their answers with a classmate using the model dialog for guidance.

OPTIONAL

Take some time to ask students about some of the movies they have seen. If possible write the movie titles on the board. For example, ask students:

- *What movie have you seen recently?*

- *How did you like it?*

PREPARE YOUR SEARCH

PAGE 35

Review the vocabulary items in the chart (types of movies and descriptions). Ask students to write the title of a movie for each type and then use a word or several words to describe each movie. Encourage them to use their own words if they want to.

OPTIONAL

After students have completed the chart, ask them to tell you about some of the items they wrote. If possible, write some of the items on the board. For example, ask students:

- *What love story have you seen recently?*

- *How was it?*

Ask students to write the titles of three English language movies that they would like to see and the type of movie each one is.

Ask students to write down the name of a movie they might like to see this weekend. Then ask them to write what type of movie it is.

> **TEACHING TIP**
>
> Walk around the classroom and have a look at students' choices. Make sure they have spelled the items correctly. Encourage students to ask you if they are unsure about the spelling of certain items.

Ask students to discuss their choices with a classmate using the model dialog as a guide.

> **LANGUAGE WINDOW**
>
> At this point it is a good idea to introduce the *Language Window* to students (see page 63 of the **Student Book** and page 56 of the **Teacher's Book**).

EXTENSION ACTIVITY

LET'S GO TO THE MOVIES

1. Photocopy the *Extension Activity* on page 57 of the **Teacher's Book.** Make one copy for each student.

2. Ask students to practice the conversation with a classmate. After they finish, ask them to change roles and practice the conversation again.

3. Ask students to complete the chart. They can use the information from *Prepare Your Search* for movie titles and types of movies.

4. Now ask students to go around the classroom and practice this conversation with four different classmates. Each time, tell students to choose a different movie, movie type, theater and time from the chart.

SEARCH THE WEB

PAGE 36

1. PREPARATION: Now that each student has chosen a movie to see, it is time for the Web search. Ask students to search for movie databases using the keywords provided in the example. When they find a database, they have to use the movie title in order to search for the movie they have chosen.

2. In order to help students select the most useful website, review the chart on page 36 of the **Student Book,** and tell students that they will need to find specific information about the movie they have chosen. Review the vocabulary items on the chart and explain any unfamiliar vocabulary.

> **NOW STUDENTS WILL USE THEIR COMPUTER AND START SEARCHING THE WEB.**

3. Ask students to open their browser and go to their favorite search engine, type their keywords and then search the Web.

Ask students to browse through the results and explore two or three different movie databases looking for the movie they have chosen.

WEB TIP

Many movie websites have links to video clips of movies. Students can view the video clips if they wish to. However, you may need to warn students that the video clips may take some time to load (depending on the size of the video clip and the student's computer). So students should be selective with which video clips they choose to view and not try and view every video clip available on a database.

Ask students to select one website and write down the movie title and the URL of the website they chose.

Ask students to read the information in the website they have chosen and complete the chart. Remind students that they should provide a reason for choosing this movie.

WEB TIP

Some movie websites are "official" sites posted by the movie company or another commercial organization. These sites contain a lot of useful information about a movie. However, these sites may also contain memorabilia with the movie logo (e.g., T-shirts, baseball caps) or other merchandise (e.g., computer screen savers, CDs, posters) that can be purchased online from those sites. Tell students that for the purposes of this lesson, they do not need to buy anything from these sites, and they should not post their credit card or other personal information on the Web.

VOCABULARY LOG

Make a copy of the *Vocabulary Log* (page 98 of the **Teacher's Book**) for each student. Ask students to select five unfamiliar words and phrases from the websites they explored and write them down in their *Vocabulary Log*. For each phrase students should provide its meaning and an example of use.

WEB TALK

PAGE 37

1. PREPARATION: Inform students that they will interview a classmate about the movie they have chosen. Review the chart with the sample questions and answers that students can use as a guide for their interview. Ask students to write their classmates' answers in the chart provided.

2. Ask students to find a partner and carry out the interview. The interviewee should consult his/her chart on page 36. If there are any students who missed the *Search the Web* session and have not completed the chart on

page 36, they can interview their partner, but they cannot be interviewed.

B

When students finish their interviews, ask them to look at their classmate's answers and answer the questions in the book.

OPTIONAL

If you have time you can ask students to share their answers with their partner, in groups or with the rest of the class.

LANGUAGE WINDOW

PAGE 63

A. Review the expressions in the *Language Window* and explain any unfamiliar vocabulary (e.g., box office hit, cool special effects).

B. Ask students to write three reasons for choosing their movie. This can also be given as homework if there is not enough time during the lesson. Review students' answers and/or ask them to compare their answers with a classmate's.

COMPUTER PROJECT

PAGE 63

1. PROJECT: Ask students to create a movie advertisement for the movie they have chosen using their word processor. Show them the sample advertisement in the book. Refer students to the *Technical Tips* (page 68 of the **Student Book**) regarding how to download pictures and text from the Web to a word processing document.

2. Remind students to list the URLs of the website(s) they used to get the pictures and information about their movie.

3. Ask students to edit the information they copied, add their own ideas, arrange the pictures and text in their document (see *Technical Tips,* page 69), check the spelling, and then save the file as *YourName*.Movie.

4. If possible ask students to make a printout of their advertisement. It may be useful to organize students to take turns when printing their projects to avoid printer jams.

SHARE YOUR PROJECT

PAGE 63

A. Ask students to E-mail their movie advertisement to three or four of their classmates.

   Steps:
   • Open their E-mail software.
   • Open a **New Message.**
   • Type the classmates' E-mail addresses on the **To:** line.
   • Type the title of the movie on the **Subject** line.
   • Write a small message such as: *Hi! Look at my movie advertisement. What do you think?*
   • Attach the advertisement (choose **Attach** or **Attachment** and then choose the advertisement file in the new window).

B. Ask students to have a look at the movie advertisements they received from their classmates and then answer the questions in their book.

C. Finally ask students to share their answers with a member of their group.

IN A TRADITIONAL CLASSROOM

If you are teaching *Internet English* in a classroom without computers, you can ask students to create a movie advertisement in class without computers.

1. Before the *Web Talk*, ask students to bring the following to class: pictures of the movie they chose from magazines (or pictures they printed from the Web), a glue stick, color markers, and blank pieces of paper or poster board.

2. Ask students to create a movie advertisement. Ask them to paste the picture(s) on the blank paper or poster board, and then use the color markers to write some information about the movie. They can use the information from their chart on page 36.

3. When students have finished their advertisement, they can post it in class.

4. Ask students to have a look at the advertisements that their classmates created and then answer the questions in **B** of *Share Your Project.*

5. Finally ask students to share their answers with a classmate.

LET'S GO TO THE MOVIES!

A **Practice this conversation with a classmate. Then change roles and practice again.**

A: What shall we do tonight?
B: Let's go to the movies.
A: What's playing?
B: Well, <u>Scream</u> is playing at the <u>Sony Theater</u> at <u>6:45</u>.
A: What kind of movie is it?
B: It's a <u>horror movie</u>.
A: Hmm. I don't like <u>horror movies</u> that much. How about a <u>love story</u>? <u>Crazy Love</u> is on at the <u>Pantheon</u>.
B: Sounds good. What time shall we go?
A: Well, the movie starts at <u>7:00</u>.
B: OK then. Let's go.

B **Complete the chart below. Write four movie titles and the type of movie for each one.**

Movie	Type	Theater	Time
Scream	horror movie	Sony Theater	6:45
Crazy Love	love story	Pantheon	7:00
1a.	1b.	CinePlaza	8:15
2a.	2b.	Grand	7:10
3a.	3b.	Piccadilly	8:50
4a.	4b.	Mega10	7:30

C **Now practice the conversation with four different classmates. Each time, use a different movie, type, theater, and time from the chart.**

Go To: file:///www.

1. **Movieweb:** Links to the movie studios and movie previews/reviews.

   http://movieweb.com/

2. **Excite Movies:** Search over 175,000 movie titles.

   http://movies.excite.com/

3. **Movie Links:** A list of links to other movie pages on the 'Net.

   http://www.movie-page.com/links.ht

4. **Webfind.net:** Searchable movie database.

   http://www.webfind.net/

5. **Internet Movie Database (IMDb):** An international organization provides cross-referenced and up-to-date movie information. Currently covers over 170,000 movies.

   http://www.imdb.com/

6. **All Movie Guide**

   http://www.allmovie.com

7. **Motion Picture Database**

   http://www.tvguide.com/movies/mopic/cgi.bin/page.c

8. **Film.com's Movie Previews:** Movie news and in-depth looks at upcoming films.

   http://www.film.com/reviews/

9. **Dark Horizons:** Movie database with news, images, reviews, trailers.

   http://www.darkhorizons.com/

Add your favorite websites for this unit here:

1. _____
2. _____
3. _____
4. _____
5. _____

UNIT 10 Vacation Abroad

IDENTIFY STUDENT BOOK, page 38	Interview classmates about their vacation preferences
PREPARE YOUR SEARCH STUDENT BOOK, page 39	Match vacation destinations and activities Choose a vacation destination and an activity to do there
SEARCH THE WEB STUDENT BOOK, page 40	Search for vacation information Put together a vacation plan
WEB TALK STUDENT BOOK, page 41	Interview a classmate about his/her vacation plan
PRACTICE PAGE STUDENT BOOK, page 64	Language Window—Talking about vacation plans Computer Project—Create a vacation brochure

KEY VOCABULARY

adventure	mountain climbing	skiing
attraction	overlook	snowboarding
beach	package tour	surfing
destination	preferences	tennis court
facilities	rainforest	tour
fishing	relax	tropical
Great Barrier Reef	resort	vacation
humid	round trip	weather
local	safari	whale watching
meet	scuba diving	youth hostel

INTRODUCTION

1. Introduce the topic to students. Tell them that this unit is about planning a vacation abroad on the Internet.
2. Now ask students to open their books. Outline the sequence of activities. Tell students that they will find out about classmates' vacation preferences; they will choose a vacation destination and activities; then they will search the Web to put together a vacation plan; finally, they will share their plan with their classmates.

PHOTO WARM-UP

PAGE 38

Ask students to have a look at the picture. Ask them questions about the picture. For example:

- *What are these people doing?*

- *Where do you think they are?*

- *Have you ever gone scuba diving? Where?*

- *What other water sports do you enjoy?*

IDENTIFY

PAGE 38

1. Before doing the questionnaire, show students the example question and answer in the book. Ask students to complete the questions.

ANSWERS

1. Do you sometimes go abroad?
2. Do you enjoy travelling by plane?
3. Do you enjoy travelling by train?
4. Do you like adventure tours?
5. Do you like tropical vacations?

2. Tell students to go around the classroom and ask these questions to their classmates. For each question they need to find a different classmate who can give a positive answer. In the end, they should have written down the names of five different students.

OPTIONAL

Take some time to ask students questions about their vacation preferences. For example, ask students:

- *Who has been abroad?*
- *Who enjoys travelling by plane?*

PREPARE YOUR SEARCH

PAGE 39

 A

Review the vocabulary items in the chart. Ask students to write a vacation destination for each activity.

POSSIBLE ANSWERS

scuba diving- Great Barrier Reef, Saipan, Hawaii, Philippines, Fiji

safari- Africa, India, South America

mountain climbing- Austria, Nepal, United States

fishing- New Zealand, Caribbean, Canada, Great Barrier Reef

surfing- Hawaii, Australia, California

skiing/snowboarding- Austria, Switzerland, United States, Canada

whale watching- Australia, Canada, United States

OPTIONAL

After students have completed the chart, ask them to provide you with some of the items they wrote. If possible, write some of the items on the board. For example, ask students:

- *Where would you go scuba diving?*
- *Where would you go for a safari?*
- *Where would be a good place for mountain climbing?*

 B

Now ask students to write down three vacation destinations they would like to visit and one activity for each.

 C

Ask students to choose one vacation destination they would like to find information about and one activity they would like to do there.

TEACHING TIP

Walk around the classroom and have a look at students' choices. Make sure they have spelled the items correctly. Encourage students to ask you if they are unsure about the spelling of certain items.

 D

Ask students to discuss their choices with a classmate using the model dialog as a guide.

LANGUAGE WINDOW

At this point it is a good idea to introduce the *Language Window* to students (see page 64 of the **Student Book** and page 62 of the **Teacher's Book**).

EXTENSION ACTIVITY

VACATION PLANS

1. Photocopy the *Extension Activity* on page 63 of the **Teacher's Book.** Make one copy for each student.

2. Ask students to practice the conversation with a classmate. After they finish, ask them to change roles and practice again.

3. Ask students to complete the chart. Tell them

to write four vacation destinations and two activities for each one.

4. Ask students to practice the conversation with four different classmates. Each time tell students to choose a different vacation destination and activities from the chart.

SEARCH THE WEB

PAGE 40

 A

1. PREPARATION: Now that each student has decided where to go for his/her vacation, it is time for the Web search. Ask students to write down the keywords for their search. Show them the example keywords in the book. Students may need to do more than one search in order to find information about activities and accommodation information in the destination they have chosen.

TEACHING TIP

Walk around the classroom and make sure that students have spelled their keywords correctly.

WEB TIP

Students can also try the travel information available in any of the popular Web directories.

2. Review the chart in **D.** Tell students that they will need to find the specific information in the chart about their vacation (e.g., dates, accommodations, activities, weather information, special attractions).

NOW STUDENTS WILL USE THEIR COMPUTER AND START SEARCHING THE WEB.

3. Ask students to open their browser and go to their favorite search engine, type their keywords, and then search the Web.

B

Ask students to browse through the results and choose a website that they like the best.

C

Ask students to write down the name and the URL of the website they chose.

D

Ask students to complete the chart with the information from the website they chose. Remind students that they have to write why they chose this vacation.

VOCABULARY LOG

Make a copy of the *Vocabulary Log* (page 98 of the **Teacher's Book**) for each student. Ask students to select five unfamiliar words and phrases from the websites they explored and write them down in their *Vocabulary Log*. For each phrase students should provide its meaning and an example of use.

WEB TALK

PAGE 41

A

1. PREPARATION: Inform students that they will interview one of their classmates about his/her vacation plan. Review the chart with the sample questions and answers that students can use as a guide for their interviews. Ask students to write their classmate's answers in the chart provided.

2. Ask students to find a classmate and carry out the interview. The interviewee should consult his/her chart on page 40 of the **Student Book.** If there are any students who missed the *Search the Web* session and have not completed the chart on page 40, they can interview a classmate, but they cannot be interviewed.

B

When students finish their interviews, ask them to look at their classmate's answers and answer the questions in the book.

OPTIONAL

If you have time you can ask students to share their answers with their partner, in groups, or with the rest of the class.

LANGUAGE WINDOW

PAGE 64

A. Review the expressions in the *Language Window*.

B. Ask students to write a few sentences about their vacation plans. This can also be given as homework if there is not enough time during the lesson. Review students' answers and/or ask them to compare their answers with a classmate's.

COMPUTER PROJECT

PAGE 64

1. PROJECT: Ask students to create a brochure for the vacation they planned using their word processor. Show them the sample brochure in the book. Refer students to the *Technical Tips* (page 68 of the **Student Book**) regarding how to download pictures and text from the Web to a word processing document.

2. Remind students to list the URL(s) of the website(s) they used to get the pictures and information about their vacation.

3. Ask students to edit the information they copied, add their own ideas, arrange the pictures and text in their document (see *Technical Tips*, page 69), check the spelling, and then save the file as *YourName*.Vacation.

4. If possible ask students to make a printout of their vacation brochure. It may be useful to organize students to take turns when printing their projects to avoid printing jams.

SHARE YOUR PROJECT

PAGE 64

A. Ask students to E-mail their brochure to three or four of their classmates.

Steps:

- Open their E-mail software.

- Open a **New Message.**
- Type the classmates' E-mail addresses on the **To:** line.
- Type the vacation destination on the **Subject** line.
- Write a small message such as: *Hi! Have a look at my vacation brochure. What do you think?*
- Attach the brochure (choose **Attach** or **Attachment** and then choose the brochure file in the new window).

B. Ask students to have a look at the vacation brochures they received from their classmates and then answer the questions in **B** of *Share Your Project*.

C. Finally, ask students to share their answers with their group.

IN A TRADITIONAL CLASSROOM

If you are teaching *Internet English* in a classroom without computers, you can ask students to create their vacation brochure in class without using computers.

1. Before the *Web Talk*, ask students to bring the following to class: pictures of their favorite vacation destination from magazines (or pictures they printed from the Web), a glue stick, color markers, and blank pieces of paper or poster board.

2. Ask students to create a vacation brochure. Ask them to paste the picture(s) on the blank paper or poster board, and then use the color markers to write some information about the vacation they chose. They can use the information from their chart on page 40 of the **Student Book.**

3. When students have finished their brochures, they can post them in class.

4. Ask students to have a look at the brochures that their classmates created and then answer the questions in **B** of *Share Your Project*.

5. Finally, ask students to share their answers with a classmate.

VACATION PLANS

A Practice this conversation with a classmate. Then change roles and practice again.

A: Do you have any plans for your summer vacation?
B: Yes. I am going to <u>Hawaii</u>.
A: What will you do there?
B: I'd like to <u>lie on the beach</u> and maybe <u>go scuba diving</u>.
A: Sounds like a great plan.
B: How about you? What are you doing this summer?
A: I think I'll go to <u>Australia</u>.
B: <u>Australia</u>? What will you do there?
A: I'll <u>visit my friends</u> and <u>go skiing</u>.
B: Cool!

B Look at the chart in the *Prepare Your Search* section on page 39 of your *Student Book.* Then write four vacation destinations and two activities for each one in the chart below.

Destination	Activity #1	Activity #2
Hawaii	lie on the beach	go scuba diving
Australia	visit friends	go skiing
1a.	1b.	1c.
2a.	2b.	2c.
3a.	3b.	3c.
4a.	4b.	4c.

C Now practice the conversation with four different classmates. Each time, use a different vacation destination and activities from the chart.

Go To: `file:///www`

1. **World Vacations:** An Internet-based provider of travel guides and hotel-related services.
    http://worldvacations.com/

2. **Online Vacation Mall:** Vacation destinations all over the world.
    http://www.onlinevacationmall.com/

3. **SkiNet.com:** Internet resource for ski gear, ski travel, ski resorts, ski instruction, etc.
    http://www.skinet.com/

4. **4Internet Network:** Vacation destinations around the world.
    http://www.4destinations.com/

5. **Funjet Vacations' Destinations:** Vacation destinations around the world.
    http://www.funjet.com/

6. **Travel and Vacations Worldwide Directory:** Vacation Index, Vacations Worldwide Directory, Activities and Destinations Index.
    http://www.vacations-ww.com/

7. **Specialty Travel:** Online index of adventure vacations and special interest travel worldwide.
    http://www.specialtytravel.com/

8. **Easy Rider Tours:** Cycling vacations in Ireland, Portugal, Spain, Prince Edward Island, Nova Scotia, and New England.
    http://www.easyridertours.com/

9. **New Adventures:** Tropical island travel, tours, vacations, hotels, scuba diving.
    http://www.newadventures.com/

10. **Vacation Land:** Packaged travel tours, hotels, airfares.
    http://www.vacation-land.com/

Add your favorite websites for this unit here:

1. _____
2. _____
3. _____
4. _____
5. _____

UNIT 11 Cyber C@fes

KEY VOCABULARY

atmosphere	design	pastry
backgammon	dessert	pop music
board games	expensive	sandwich
business hours	fee	selection
cappuccino	friendly	snack
chess	gift shop	soup
coffee shop	hang out	surf the Web
computer games	Internet cafe	tap into
cost	juice	tea
cyber cafe	offer	training

INTRODUCTION

1. Introduce the topic to students. Tell them that this unit is about cyber cafes, i.e., coffee shops with computers connected to the Internet.

2. Now ask students to open their books. Outline the sequence of activities. Tell students that they will talk about different things to do at a cyber cafe; then they will choose a country in which to find a cyber cafe; next they will search the Web and collect information about a cyber cafe; and finally they will talk about their cyber cafe with a classmate.

PHOTO WARM-UP

PAGE 42

1. Ask students to have a look at the picture of the cyber cafe. Explain what a cyber cafe is.

2. Ask students questions about the picture. For example, ask students:

   • *Do you think the people in the cyber cafe are having fun?*

   • *Are there any cyber cafes in your city?*

   • *Have you ever been to a cyber cafe?*

PAGE 42

A

Review the list of activities to do at a cyber cafe and then ask students to check they ones they would do.

B

PAIR WORK: When students have finished writing, ask them to compare their answers with a classmate using the model dialog for guidance.

OPTIONAL

Take some time to ask students questions about the activities they checked. For example, ask students:

- *Who would like to surf the Web?*

- *Who would like to send or check E-mail?*

PREPARE YOUR SEARCH

PAGE 43

A

1. Ask students to have a look at the chart. Review the vocabulary items in the chart.

2. Ask students to complete the blanks on the map.

POSSIBLE ANSWERS

surf the Web–find information about restaurants, do some online shopping, send a Web card, register for an English course abroad, do some English quizzes on the Web

E-mail–read new messages, reply to E-mail messages

computer games–blackjack, golf, chess, war games, Quake, Doom, Starseige, Half-life

hang out at the cafe–have a snack, meet friends, watch TV/video clips, listen to live music

OPTIONAL

After students have completed the chart, ask them to provide you with some of the items they wrote. If possible, write some of the items on the board. For example, ask students:

- *What are some things you can do on the Web?*

- *What are some computer games you can play at a cyber cafe?*

WEB TIP

Explain to students that cyber cafes are very useful when they go travelling because they can go to a cyber cafe and send E-mail to their family and friends to keep in touch. They can also surf the Web for information on things to do in the city they are visiting.

B

Ask students to write down three things they would most like to do at a cyber cafe abroad.

C

Have students choose a country in which they would like to find a cyber cafe.

TEACHING TIP

Walk around the classroom and have a look at students' choices. Make sure they have spelled the items correctly. Encourage students to ask you if they are unsure about the spelling of certain items.

D

Ask students to discuss their choices with a classmate using the model dialog as a guide.

LANGUAGE WINDOW

At this point it is a good idea to introduce the *Language Window* to students, see page 65 of the **Student Book** and page 68 of the **Teacher's Book**.

EXTENSION ACTIVITY

AT THE CYBER CAFE

1. Photocopy the *Extension Activity* on page 69 of the **Teacher's Book.** Make one copy for each student.

2. Ask students to practice the conversation with a classmate. After they finish, ask them to change roles and practice the conversation again.

3. Ask students to complete the chart. Tell them to write two activities for each cafe.

4. Ask students to practice the conversation with three different classmates. Each time, tell students to choose a different cafe and activities from the chart.

SEARCH THE WEB

PAGE 44

A

1. PREPARATION: Now that each student has decided where to find a cyber cafe, it is time for the Web search. Tell students to use the country they have chosen and *cyber cafe* or *Internet cafe* as keywords for their search, as in the example in the book. Ask them to write down their keywords.

> **TEACHING TIP**
> Walk around the classroom and make sure that students have spelled their keywords correctly.

2. In order to help students choose the most useful website, review the chart in **D**, explain any unfamiliar vocabulary, and tell students that they will need to find this specific information about a cyber cafe.

   NOW STUDENTS WILL USE THEIR COMPUTER AND START SEARCHING THE WEB.

3. Ask students to open their browser and go to their favorite search engine, type their keywords and then search the Web.

> **WEB TIP**
> If students have trouble finding a cyber cafe in the city they have chosen, you can direct them to the cyber cafe guides in the *Useful URLs* list on page 70 of the **Teacher's Book.**

B

Ask students to browse through the results and explore two or three of the cyber cafes.

C

Ask students to choose the cyber cafe that interests them the most and write down the name of the cafe and the URL of the website they chose.

D

Ask students to read the information about the cyber cafe they chose and complete the chart.

> **TEACHING TIP**
> Students may have difficulty filling in all the sections in the chart. Tell them that they should explore all the pages in the cyber cafe website and collect as much of the information on the chart as possible.

> **VOCABULARY LOG**
> Make a copy of the *Vocabulary Log* (page 98 of the **Teacher's Book**) for each student. Ask students to select five unfamiliar words and phrases from the websites they explored and write them down in their *Vocabulary Log*. For each phrase students should provide its meaning and an example of use.

WEB TALK

PAGE 45

A

1. PREPARATION: Inform students that they will interview a classmate about the cyber cafe they found. Review the chart with the sample questions and answers that students can use as a guide for their interviews. Ask students to write their classmate's answers in the chart provided.

2. Ask students to find a partner and carry out the interview. The interviewee should consult his/her chart on page 44 of the **Student Book.** If there are any students who missed the *Search the Web* session and have not completed the chart on page 44, they can interview their classmate, but they cannot be interviewed.

B

When students finish their interviews, ask them to look at their classmate's answers and answer the questions in the book.

If you have time you can ask students to share their answers with their partner, in groups, or with the rest of the class.

LANGUAGE WINDOW

PAGE 65

A. Review the expressions in the *Language Window*.

B. Ask students to write their own examples. This can also be given as homework if there is not enough time during the lesson. Review students' answers and/or ask them to compare their answers with a classmate.

COMPUTER PROJECT

PAGE 65

1. PROJECT: Ask students to create a brochure for their favorite cyber cafe using their word processor. Show them the sample brochure in the book. Refer students to the *Technical Tips* (page 68 of the **Student Book**) regarding how to download pictures and text from the Web to a word processing document.

2. Remind students to list the URL(s) of the website(s) they used to get the pictures and information about their cyber cafe.

3. Ask students to edit the information they copied, add their own ideas, arrange the pictures and text in their document (see *Technical Tips*, page 69), check the spelling, and then save the file as *YourName*.cafe.

4. If possible ask students to make a printout of their cyber cafe brochure. It may be useful to organize students to take turns when printing their projects to avoid printing jams.

SHARE YOUR PROJECT

PAGE 65

A. Ask students to E-mail their cyber cafe brochure to three or four of their classmates.

Steps:
- Open their E-mail software.
- Open a **New Message.**
- Type the classmates' E-mail addresses on the **To:** line.
- Type name of the cyber cafe and the city it is in on the **Subject** line.
- Write a small message such as: *Hi! Have a look at my cyber cafe. What do you think?*
- Attach the brochure (choose **Attach** or **Attachment** and then choose the cyber cafe brochure file in the new window).

B. Ask students to have a look at the brochures they received from their classmates and then answer the questions in their book.

C. Finally ask students to share their answers with their group.

IN A TRADITIONAL CLASSROOM

If you are teaching *Internet English* in a classroom without computers, you can ask students to create their cyber cafe brochure in class without using computers.

1. Before the *Web Talk*, ask students to bring the following to class: pictures of a cyber cafe from magazines (or pictures they printed from the Web), a glue stick, color markers, and blank pieces of paper or poster board.

2. Ask students to create a brochure. Ask them to paste the picture(s) on the blank paper or poster board, and then use the color markers to write some information about the cyber cafe. They can use the information from their chart on page 44.

3. When students have finished their brochures, they can post them in class

4. Ask students to have a look at the brochures that their classmates created and then answer the questions in **B** of *Share Your Project*.

5. Finally, ask students to share their answers with a classmate.

A Practice this conversation with a classmate. Then change roles and practice again.

> **A:** What did you do yesterday afternoon?
>
> **B:** I went to <u>CyberWorld</u>.
>
> **A:** What did you do there?
>
> **B:** I <u>found some information about new movies</u> and I <u>checked my E-mail</u>.

B Look at the chart on page 43 of your *Student Book.* Then write down two different activities you could do for each of the cyber cafes in the chart below.

Cyber Cafe	Activity #1	Activity #2
CyberWorld	find information about new movies	check E-mail
NetHub	1a.	1b.
CyberShack	2a.	2b.
NetCafe	3a.	3b.
Cyberland	4a.	4b.

C Now practice the conversation with four different classmates. Each time, use a different cyber cafe and activities from the chart.

Go To: `file:///www`

1. **International Internet cafe guide:** Locate a cyber cafe worldwide.
   http://www.tempestcom.com/cafelocate.htm

2. **Cybercafes - Internet Cafes - Cyber cafe Guide:** List of cyber cafes worldwide.
   http://www.cyberhost4.com/netcafeg/

3. **Cybercafe Search Engine:** Cyber cafe directory: search by city, state or country.
   http://www.cybercaptive.com/

4. **2b Cyber Cafe Directory:** Directory of cyber cafes based in the U.K.
   http://www.2b.co.uk/cybercafes/

5. **Global Cybercafe Guide:** Directory of cyber cafes around the world.
   http://www.sbds.net/cafes/

6. **The CyberCafe Guide:** Directory of cyber cafes around the world.
   http://www.cyber-star.com/cyberlocate.html

7. **NetCafe Guide:** Cyber cafes, Internet cafes, 1,500 cafes worldwide in cyber cafe guide.
   http://netcafeguide.com/

8. **Yahoo!** Yahoo!'s complete listing of cyber cafes around the world.
   http://dir.yahoo.com/Business_and_Economy/Companies/Internet_Services/
   Internet_Cafes/Complete_Listing/

9. **Global:** Directory of cyber cafes in the US.
   http://www.globalcomputing.com/cafes.html

10. **Gnomon Publishing:** Australian Internet cafe and net access guide.
    http://www.gnomon.com.au/publications/netaccess/

11. **Euro Cybercafes:** Directory of cyber cafes in Europe.
    http://eyesite.simplenet.com/eurocybercafes/

Add your favorite websites for this unit here:

1. _____

2. _____

3. _____

4. _____

5. _____

Working Abroad

IDENTIFY STUDENT BOOK, page 46	Match jobs with workplaces
PREPARE YOUR SEARCH STUDENT BOOK, page 47	Complete a chart about jobs, skills, and personal qualities Choose a type of job and a country to work in
SEARCH THE WEB STUDENT BOOK, page 48	Search for job databases Collect information about a job
WEB TALK STUDENT BOOK, page 49	Role-play a job interview
PRACTICE PAGE STUDENT BOOK, page 66	Language Window—Expressing skills and abilities Computer Project—Create a job advertisement

KEY VOCABULARY

Alpine resort	description	language teacher	salary
applicant	designer	lifeguard	seasonal
apply	drawing	maintenance	skiing
art teacher	earn	nanny	skill
artistic	employment	office worker	summer camp
athletic	energetic	opportunity	swimming pool
camp counselor	filing	outgoing	talkative
career	flight attendant	painting	telemarketer
carving	foreign language	patient	typing
classifieds	(be) good at	personal qualities	Web graphics
college education	hardworking	polite	well-organized
convince	helper	private home	work experience
cook	instructor	reliable	workplace
creative	job listings	responsible	
deadline	kitchen	restaurant	

INTRODUCTION

1. Introduce the topic to students. Tell them that this unit is about finding jobs on the Internet.
2. Now ask students to open their books. Outline the sequence of activities. Tell students that they will talk about different jobs and workplaces; then they will identify their skills and personal qualities; next they will choose a job and a country to work in; after that they will search the Web for jobs; and finally they will role-play a job interview.

WEB PAGE WARM-UP

PAGE 46

Ask students to have a look at the picture. Ask students questions about the picture. For example, ask students:

- *Where are these people?*

- *What kind of work do you think they do?*

- *What do you think they are talking about?*

- *Would you like to work abroad? Why or why not?*

PAGE 46

Review the vocabulary (*Jobs* and *Workplaces*) and then ask students to match each of the jobs with a workplace.

ANSWERS
1. ski instructor– b. at Alpine resorts
2. nanny– c. in private homes
3. camp counselor– e. at summer camps
4. language teacher– f. at universities and schools
5. cook– d. in restaurant kitchens
6. lifeguard– a. at beaches and swimming pools

PAIR WORK: When students have finished writing, ask them to compare their answers with a classmate's using the model dialog for guidance.

OPTIONAL

Take some time to ask students about their answers. For example, ask students:

- *Where does a ski instructor work?*
- *Would you like to work as a ski instructor?*

PREPARE YOUR SEARCH

PAGE 47

1. Review the vocabulary items in the chart and explain any unfamiliar vocabulary.
2. Ask students to complete the chart with words from the box.

ANSWERS
1. using computers, filing
2. creative, energetic
3. cook's helper
4. skiing, giving instructions
5. outgoing, talkative
6. flight attendant

OPTIONAL

After students have completed the chart, confirm their answers. For example, ask students:

- *What skills does an office worker need?*
- *What personal qualities does a children's art teacher need?*

Now ask students to write down three skills and three personal qualities that they have.

Tell students to choose a type of job that they would like, and a country where they would like to work.

TEACHING TIP

Walk around the classroom and have a look at students' answers. Make sure they have spelled the items correctly. Encourage students to ask you if they are unsure about the spelling of certain items.

Ask students to discuss their choices with a classmate using the model dialog as a guide.

LANGUAGE WINDOW

At this point it is a good idea to introduce the *Language Window* (see page 66 of the **Student Book** and page 74 of the **Teacher's Book**).

EXTENSION ACTIVITY

JOB INTERVIEW

1. Photocopy the *Extension Activity* on page 75 of the **Teacher's Book.** Make one copy for each student.
2. Ask students to practice the conversation with a classmate. After they finish, ask them to change roles and practice again.
3. Ask students to complete the chart. For each job tell them to write two skills and two personal qualities.
4. Ask students to practice the conversation five more times with five different classmates. Each time they should choose a different job and job information from the chart.

SEARCH THE WEB

PAGE 48

1. PREPARATION: Now that each student has chosen a job and a country to work in, it is time for the Web search. Tell students they will be looking for job databases. For keywords they can use *summer jobs*, *student jobs*, or the job and country they chose as keywords. You can also direct students to the employment links in their favorite Web directory.

> **TEACHING TIP**
> Walk around the classroom and make sure that students have spelled their keywords correctly.

2. In order to help students choose the most useful website, review the chart on page 48, and tell students that they will need to find specific information about a job in order to complete the chart.

 NOW STUDENTS WILL USE THEIR COMPUTER AND START SEARCHING THE WEB.

3. Ask students to open their browser and go to their favorite search engine, type their keywords, and then search the Web.

B

Ask students to browse through the results and explore different job databases for jobs they like.

> **WEB TIP**
> Most job databases are searchable (i.e., students can search the database using the job they want as a keyword). Other databases allow searches with the city and/or country as keywords. Also, if any students cannot find information about the job they chose, tell them to use as many different synonyms of the job they are looking for as possible. If a student is looking for a job as a 'nanny', but cannot find one, then he/she can do additional searches using synonyms or near synonyms of the word nanny, such as *au pair, babysitter, child care*.

C

Tell students to choose a job they like and write down the name of the job, the database, and the URL.

D

Ask students to read the job information and complete the chart.

> **VOCABULARY LOG**
> Make a copy of the *Vocabulary Log* (page 98 of the **Teacher's Book**) for each student. Ask students to select five unfamiliar words and phrases from the websites they explored and write them down in their *Vocabulary Log*. For each phrase students should provide its meaning and an example of use.

WEB TALK

PAGE 49

A

1. PREPARATION: Inform students that they will role-play a job interview with a classmate. Ask each student to make a copy of the job information in the chart on page 49 and give it to his/her partner. Then review the sample questions and answers that students can use as a guide for their interviews. Ask students to write their classmate's answers in the chart provided.

2. Now ask each pair to decide who will play the interviewer and who will play the job applicant. Then ask them to read the role-play instructions for Interviewer and Job Applicant and carry out the interview.

B

After students finish their interview, they should change roles and practice it again. If there are any students who missed the *Search the Web* session, they can interview their classmates, but they cannot be interviewed. When students finish their interviews, ask them to look at their classmate's answers and answer the questions in the book.

If you have time you can ask students to share their charts and answers in groups or with the rest of the class.

LANGUAGE WINDOW

PAGE 66

A. Review the ways to express skills, abilities, personal qualities, and experience in the *Language Window*.

B. Ask students to write down some of their skills, abilities, personal qualities, and experience. This can also be given as homework if there is not enough time during the lesson. Review students' answers and/or ask them to compare their answers with a classmate's.

COMPUTER PROJECT

PAGE 66

1. PROJECT: Ask students to create an advertisement about the job they researched using their word processor. Show them the sample job advertisement in the book. Refer students to the *Technical Tips* (page 68 of the **Student Book**) regarding how to download pictures and text from the Web to a word processing document.

2. Remind students to list the URL(s) of the website(s) they used to get the pictures and information about their job advertisement.

3. Ask students to edit the information they copied, add their own ideas, arrange the pictures and text in their document (see *Technical Tips*, page 69), check the spelling, and then save the file as *YourName*.Job.

4. If possible ask students to make a printout of their job advertisement. It may be useful to organize students to take turns when printing their projects to avoid printing jams.

SHARE YOUR PROJECT

PAGE 66

A. Ask students to E-mail their job advertisement to three or four of their classmates.

Steps:
- Open their E-mail software.
- Open a **New Message.**
- Type the classmates' E-mail addresses on the **To:** line.
- Type the job title on the **Subject** line.
- Write a small message such as: *Hi! Have a look at my job advertisement. What do you think?*
- Attach the advertisement (choose **Attach** or **Attachment** and then choose the job advertisement file in the new window).

B. Ask students to have a look at the job advertisements they received from their classmates and then answer the questions in their book.

C. Finally, ask students to share their answers with their group.

IN A TRADITIONAL CLASSROOM

If you are teaching *Internet English* in a classroom without computers, you can ask students to create their job advertisement in class without using computers.

1. Before the *Web Talk*, ask students to bring the following to class: pictures related to the job from magazines (or pictures they printed from the Web), a glue stick, color markers, and blank pieces of paper or poster board.

2. Ask students to create their job advertisement. Ask them to paste the picture(s) on the blank paper or poster board and then use the color markers to write the information about the job. They can use the information from the chart on page 48 of the **Student Book.**

3. When students have finished their advertisements, they can post them in class

4. Ask students to have a look at the job advertisements that their classmates created and then answer the questions in **B** of *Share Your Project*.

5. Finally, ask students to share their answers with a classmate.

JOB INTERVIEW

A Practice this conversation with a classmate. Then change roles and practice again.

Interviewer:	I would like to ask you a few questions.
Applicant:	Of course. Go right ahead.
Interviewer:	What position are you applying for?
Applicant:	I'm applying for the **flight attendant** position.
Interviewer:	What skills do you have?
Applicant:	I'm good at **speaking English**.
Interviewer:	And what is your best quality?
Applicant:	I'm **friendly**.

B Look at the chart in Part A on page 47 of your *Student Book.* Then write a skill and a personal quality suitable for each job in the chart below.

Jobs	Skills	Personal Qualities
flight attendant	speaking English	friendly
office worker	1a.	1b.
diving instructor	2a.	2b.
salesperson	3a.	3b.
art teacher	4a.	4b.
lifeguard	5a.	5b.

C Now practice the conversation with five different classmates. Each time, use a different job, skill, and personal quality from the chart.

Working Abroad
Useful URLs

Go To: `file:///www`

1. **Summer Jobs:** Database of seasonal and part-time jobs worldwide.
   http://www.summerjobs.com/

2. **Great Summer Jobs:** Job opportunities at summer camps in the US and selected countries abroad.
   http://gsj.petersons.com/

3. **Cool Works:** Summer jobs & winter jobs in great places: ski resorts, national parks, ranches, cruise ships, even Alaskan fishing camps.
   http://www.coolworks.com/

4. **AllSearchEngines.Com:** Listings of all the major Internet career and job search engines, meta search engines and directories.
   http://www.allsearchengines.com/careerjobs.html

5. **+Jobs International:** Worldwide Internet job links database.
   http://www.plusjobs.com/

6. **JOBS ONLINE:** Job database for jobs in the US.
   http://www.jobs-online.net/

7. **4Work:** Lists job opportunities across the US, updated daily.
   http://www.4work.com/

8. **IDIWA:** Dive jobs for scuba diving instructors and dive professionals.
   http://divejobs.com/

9. **The World Wide Web Employment Office:** Job database for jobs in the US.
   http://www.employmentoffice.net/

10. **Employment Opportunities Australia:** Australian/Asian jobs search database with Australian and Asian Employment opportunities for all professionals.
    http://employment.com.au/index.html

Add your favorite websites for this unit here:

1. _____

2. _____

3. _____

4. _____

5. _____

UNIT 13 — News Online

KEY VOCABULARY

academic	economy	news	radio
accident	entrance examinations	newspaper	reporter
art	graduate	online	science
become	happen	paragraph	service
body	headline	pass	source
business	healthy	passion	stay
centenarian	high school	politics	summary
continue	law	primary	take place
current events	lead	school	technology
degree	lecture	print master	trading company
details	magazine	probably	TV
doctorate	manager	publish	world

INTRODUCTION

1. Introduce the topic to students. Tell them that this unit is about using an online news service (i.e., getting the news through the Internet).

2. Now ask students to open their books. Outline the sequence of activities. Tell students that they will identify different ways of getting the news; then they will read a news story and answer questions about it; next they will search the Web for news links and choose a news story to read; and finally they will interview a classmate about his/her news story.

WEB PAGE WARM-UP

PAGE 50

Ask students to have a look at the picture of the BBC World Service Web page. Ask them questions about the picture. For example, ask students:

- *Are you interested in sports? Which ones?*

- *How do you usually get your sports news?*

- *Are you interested in sports in other countries?*

- *Which links on this Web page would you like to click on?*

IDENTIFY

PAGE 50

Review the different ways of getting the news and explain any unfamiliar vocabulary. Ask students to write down how frequently they use each way using a suitable frequency phrase from the box or one of their own.

PAIR WORK: When students have finished writing, ask them to compare their answers with a classmate using the model dialog for guidance.

OPTIONAL

Take some time to ask students questions about the different ways of getting the news. For example, ask students:

- *Who likes to watch the news on TV?*
- *How often do you watch the news on TV?*

PREPARE YOUR SEARCH

PAGE 51

Ask students to answer the questions about education in their country. In **2c** put students in pairs to share their reasons.

Ask students to read the news story. Tell them that it is a story about a 96-year-old man about to start studying for a university degree. Explain any unfamiliar vocabulary (e.g., centenarian, doctorate).

After students have finished reading the story, ask them to match each of the parts of the story with the correct definition.

> **ANSWERS**
>
> **Lead:** This is the first paragraph of the news story.
>
> **Headline:** This is the title of the story.
>
> **Body:** This part gives more information and details about the story.

> **TEACHING TIP**
>
> You should explain to students the inverted pyramid structure of a news story, i.e., most of the important information is at the beginning of the news story and the less important details are towards the end of the news story. Each news story answers five basic questions: Who? What? Where? When? Why?

Now ask students to read the story again and complete the answers to the five basic questions.

> **SUGGESTED ANSWERS**
>
> 1. It's about Mr. Toyokuni Utagawa (a famous Japanese print master).
> 2. A 96-year-old man passed the difficult entrance examinations for Kinki University.
> 3. In Japan.
> 4. Last Monday.
> 5. Because he wants to become the first centenarian to complete a doctorate degree in law.

OPTIONAL

After students have answered the questions, ask them to provide you with their answers. If possible, write the answers on the board.

> **LANGUAGE WINDOW**
>
> At this point it is a good idea to introduce the *Language Window* (see page 67 of the **Student Book** and page 80 of the **Teacher's Book**).

EXTENSION ACTIVITY

NEWS ONLINE

1. Photocopy the *Extension Activity* on page 81 of the **Teacher's Book.** Make one copy for each student.

2. Explain to students that when we read the news online, we usually look at the news items and choose to read only those items that look interesting. Ask students to look at the news items and write the two that interest them the most.

3. Ask students to write why they think the stories are interesting in **B**.

4. Tell students to think of two things they would like to find out for each story and then write a question for each story in **C**. Students can use the *Language Window*, page 67 of the **Student Book**, or the sample wh-questions in the *Prepare Your Search* section, page 51 of the **Student Book**, as models for their questions.

5. Ask students to compare their choices and questions with a classmate's.

SEARCH THE WEB

PAGE 52

1. PREPARATION: Tell students they will look for a news story on the Web using the news links on their favorite Web directory. Show them the example links in the book. Tell them that after they find a news site, they should choose a news story category and then choose one story to read. Show them the example categories in the book.

2. Review the chart in **D** and tell students that they will need to find this kind of specific information about their news story.

> 🖱 **NOW STUDENTS WILL USE THEIR COMPUTER AND START SEARCHING THE WEB.**

3. Ask students to open their browser and go to their favorite Web directory. Tell them to locate the news links that the Web directory provides.

> **WEB TIP**
>
> If students search for magazine or newspaper websites, they should be aware that a large number of well-known newspapers and magazines require subscription to search their websites. These sites could require payment of fees, so it is a good idea to avoid them.

Ask students to browse through the news categories and choose a news story to read.

Ask students to write down the story headline and the URL of the website they chose.

Ask students to read the news story they chose and fill in as much of the chart as they can.

> **VOCABULARY LOG**
>
> Make a copy of the *Vocabulary Log* (page 98 of the **Teacher's Book**) for each student. Ask students to select five unfamiliar words and phrases from the websites they explored and write them down in their *Vocabulary Log*. For each phrase students should provide its meaning and an example of use.

WEB TALK

PAGE 53

PREPARATION: Inform students that they will interview a classmate about his/her news story. Review the sample questions and answers that students can use as a guide for their interviews. Tell students they will write their classmate's answers in the chart provided.

Ask students to find a partner and ask, "What is your story about?" Then have students write their answer in the space provided.

Tell students to now continue the interview by asking specific wh-questions about the news story and writing their classmates' answers in the *Interview Notes* chart. The interviewee should consult his/her chart on page 52 of the **Student Book.** If there are any students who missed the *Search the Web* session and have not completed the chart on page 52, they can interview a classmate, but they cannot be interviewed.

When students finish their interviews, ask them to look at their classmate's answers in their chart and decide which story is the most interesting. Then ask students to explain their reasons to their partner.

LANGUAGE WINDOW

PAGE 67

A. Review the expressions in the *Language Window*. Main points:

- Simple Past Tense
- Questions with Who, What, Where, When, and Why

B. Ask students to write their own examples of wh-questions in the past tense about the news story they chose. This can also be given as homework if there is not enough time during the lesson. Review students' answers and/or ask them to compare their answers with a classmate's.

COMPUTER PROJECT

PAGE 67

1. PROJECT: Ask students to write a summary of the news story they chose using their word processor. Show them the sample summary in the book. Tell students that they are free to add images from the Web to their summary. Refer students to the *Technical Tips* (page 68 of the **Student Book**) regarding how to download pictures and text from the Web to a word processing document.

2. Remind students to list the URL(s) of the website(s) they used to get any pictures and the information for their summary.

3. Ask students to create a summary of the news story based on the information they gathered in the *My News Story* chart on page 52 of the **Student Book.** Ask students to arrange the pictures (if they used any) and the text in their document, check the spelling, and then save the file as *YourName.*News.

4. If possible ask students to make a printout of their summary. It may be useful to organize students to take turns when printing their projects to avoid printing jams.

SHARE YOUR PROJECT

PAGE 67

A. Ask students to E-mail their summary to three or four of their classmates.

Steps:

- Open their E-mail software.
- Open a **New Message.**
- Type the classmates' E-mail address on the **To:** line.
- Type the title of the news story on the **Subject** line.
- Write a small message such as: *Hi! Have a look at my news story summary. What do you think?*
- Attach the summary (choose **Attach** or **Attachment** and then choose the summary file in the new window).

B. Ask students to have a look at the summaries they received from their classmates and then answer the questions in their book.

C. Finally, ask students to share their answers with a classmate.

IN A TRADITIONAL CLASSROOM

If you are teaching *Internet English* in a classroom without computers, you can ask students to create their summary in class without using computers.

1. Before the *Web Talk*, ask students to bring the following to class: pictures related to their news story from magazines or newspapers (or pictures they printed from the Web), a glue stick, color markers, and blank pieces of paper or poster board.

2. Ask students to create a summary of the news story they chose. Ask them to paste the picture(s) on the blank paper or poster board, and then write the news summary. They can use the information from their chart in **D** on page 52 of the **Student Book.**

3. When students have finished their summaries, they can post them in class.

4. Ask students to have a look at some of the summaries that their classmates created and then answer the questions in **B** of *Share Your Project*.

5. Finally, ask students to share their answers with a classmate.

NEWS LINKS

World News
- Amazon Rainforest Update
- Parents Press for Gun Control
- Exercise Helps Smokers Quit

Science
- International Space Station
- Recent UFO Sightings
- Air Inside Cars Found Dirtier Than Outside

Business
- Signs of an Improved Global Economy
- Electronic Commerce: Millions of Transactions Every Day
- Internet Stocks

Sports
- NBA Finals
- U.S. Favored to Win Women's World Cup
- Switzerland Gets Ready for the Olympics in 2006

Technology
- FBI Investigates Recent Computer "Worm" Virus
- Computer Hackers Attack Government Web Site
- Smart Cars Could Help Drivers Avoid Accidents

Entertainment
- Restaurant Guide
- New Movie Releases
- This Week's Top Ten CDs

A Read through the news items above. Then choose the two that interest you the most and write them on the lines provided.

News Item #1 _____

News Item #2 _____

B Why do you think these news items are interesting? Write one reason for each.

Example: Smart Cars Could Help Drivers Avoid Accidents
I think "smart cars" are a wonderful idea.

News Item #1 _____

News Item #2 _____

C Write a question you would like to know the answer to for each news item.

Example: Smart Cars Could Help Drivers Avoid Accidents
How much does a smart car cost?

News Item #1 _____

News Item #2 _____

D Share your answers with a classmate.

Go To: `file:///www.`

You can find links to news sites in most Internet portals. Here are some:

1. **Yahoo!** Extensive list of links to the latest news stories.

   http://headlines.yahoo.com/Full_Coverage/

2. **Yahoo!** Directory of USA newspapers.

   http://dir.yahoo.com/News_and_Media/Newspapers/

3. **ABC News**

   http://abcnews.go.com/index.html

4. **Lycos**

   http://www.lycos.com/news/

5. **Excite**

   http://nt.excite.com/news

Other websites:

6. **Newsrack:** Online newspapers and magazines of the world - A newsstand-type listing of international newspaper and magazine sites.

   http://www.newsrack.com/

7. **CPNet:** The College Press Network - Index of online student newspapers.

   http://www.cpnet.com/college/newspapers.htm

8. **Auburn University Libraries:** A list of nearly 1,750 electronic newspapers available on the Web.

   http://www.lib.auburn.edu/madd/docs/newspapers/newspapers.list2.html

9. **CNN**

   http://cnn.com

ATTENTION: A large number of well-known newspapers and magazines require subscription before allowing you to search their websites. Subscription to these sites could require payment of fees, so it is a good idea to avoid them.

Add your favorite websites for this unit here:

1. _____

2. _____

3. _____

4. _____

5. _____

Internet English Tests

There are four tests for *Internet English*

- Test 1 covers Units 1, 2, and 3.

- Test 2 covers Units 4, 5, and 6.

- Test 3 covers Units 7, 8, and 9.

- Test 4 covers Units 10, 11, 12, and 13.

Contents

- Each test has activities (e.g., matching exercises, open-ended questions, reading comprehension exercises, fill-in-the-blank exercises, scrambled conversations) that cover the computer skills, vocabulary, and language structures dealt with in each set of units.

- Students complete each test in writing, i.e., they do not need to use a computer in order to complete the tests.

Preparation

- At the end of each set of units make one copy of the corresponding test for each student.

- Ask students to make sure they write their name at the top of the test.

- Tell students they have to answer all the questions in the test.

- Give students enough time to complete the test (approximately 35–45 minutes).

Marking the Test

- First, the teacher must mark the sections with answers that vary.

- You can ask students to mark the remaining sections of a partner's test.

- Use the answer key and go through the test one item at a time.

- Have students use a different colored pen for checking and correcting their partners' answers.

- Ask students to circle or check correct answers.

- Incorrect answers should be crossed out and the correct answer should be written down.

- After all answers have been checked, students should write down the total number of points for the sections they corrected. Tell them to give one point for each correct answer unless otherwise marked. Make sure students understand that the example answers do not count as correct answers.

- Each test has a maximum of 50 points. To convert a score into a percentage multiply the total points by two (e.g., 50 points x 2 = 100%).

- Allow students some time to go through their own test, note their mistakes, and record their score.

General Notes

- Have students complete the test in class.

- Don't let students keep the test or make a copy of it. This way you can re-use the tests with different groups of students.

- With open-ended questions, you have to decide whether you want your students to provide full answers or short answers, and whether spelling and punctuation mistakes count.

TEST 1: UNITS 1–3

(A) **Match the terms on the left with their definitions on the right.**   (____ / 10 points)

1. __d__ file
2. ____ window
3. ____ menu
4. ____ Print
5. ____ word processor
6. ____ highlight
7. ____ Save As
8. ____ Cut and Paste
9. ____ icon
10. ____ New
11. ____ click

a. Press and release the button on the mouse
b. Select text/images with the mouse
c. A small picture or symbol
d. Text or other data stored together with a special name
e. A list of computer operations
f. This command creates a new file.
g. Software for creating text files
h. A box on the screen that displays text/images
i. This command saves a file under a different name.
j. This command sends the contents of a file to the printer.
k. These commands move text/images from one place to another.

(B) **Write a short E-mail message introducing yourself to your classmates. Include your name, age, hometown, hobbies, and reason for studying English.**   (____ / 10 points)

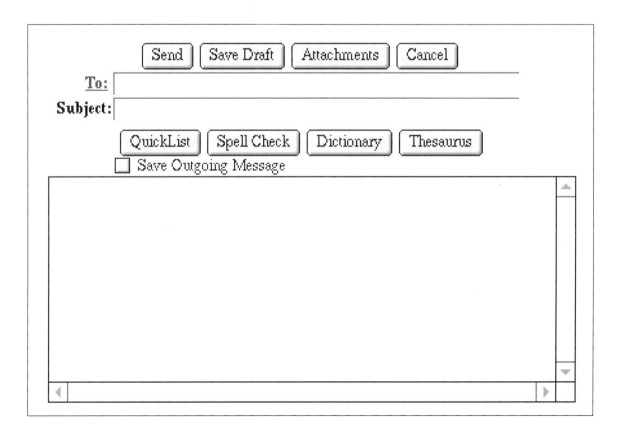

C **Answer the following questions about yourself.**   (____ / 5 points)

1. How often do you use computers?

    _____

2. What is your E-mail address?

    _____

3. How often do you check your E-mail?

    _____

4. How often do you surf the Web?

    _____

5. Name something you would like to do on the Internet.

    _____

D **Read the following passage and answer the questions.**   (____ / 10 points)

> The Internet is a network of millions of computers. They are linked together by phone lines, fiberoptic cables, satellite, and microwave connections. The United States Department of Defense started the Internet in 1969, but today nobody owns or controls it. Use of the Internet, and the part of the Internet called the World Wide Web, has been growing dramatically.
>
> The World Wide Web, usually called "the Web," is the part of the Internet where millions of Web pages containing text, images, and sound from people all over the world are connected. A typical Web page looks like a magazine page, but with your mouse you can click on "live" areas on the page called links to go to a different Web page. The Web has become the most popular area on the Internet. You can easily get on the Web by using software called a Web browser. Two of the most popular are Netscape Navigator™ and Internet Explorer™.
>
> You can use the Web for research, business, entertainment, or personal interests. Some specific things people do on the Web are send E-mail, go shopping, find jobs, get the latest news, order a meal, and make travel plans. And the list gets longer every day!

1. What is the Internet?

    _____

2. How are the computers linked together?

    _____

3. Who started the Internet? When?

    _____

4. Who controls the Internet?

    _____

5. What does "WWW" stand for?

    _____

Name _____

6. What does a typical Web page look like?

_____

7. What happens when you click on links?

_____

8. What is the most popular part of the Internet?

_____

9. Name the two most popular Web browsers.

_____

10. From the reading, name two specific things you can do on the Web.

_____

(E) Unscramble the E-mail message. Write a number from 2 to 11 in front of each sentence in the order you think is correct. The first sentence is numbered for you.   _____ / 10 points

_____ because I have to buy my train tickets early.

_____ bye for now,

_____ going to visit you in Tokyo next weekend.

__1__ Hi Jun!

_____ Hotels in Tokyo are very expensive, though. Could I

_____ How are you? I am very happy because

_____ Kim :-)

_____ I just finished my exams!

_____ Please let me know soon,

_____ stay at your house?

_____ They were so difficult! To relax now, I'm thinking of

(F) Choose the best keywords for each situation. Circle your choices below.   _____ / 5 points

1. You want to find Web pages that contain the keyword Seiko in the URL.
   a. title:Seiko   b. url:Seiko   c. Seiko

2. You want to find information about computers but not about iMacs.
   a. "iMac computers"   b. title:computers   c. computers -iMac

3. You want to find websites containing the phrase Basic HTML.
   a. "Basic HTML"   b. Basic HTML   c. url:Basic HTML

4. You want to find Web pages containing the keyword Hilton in the title.
   a. url:Hilton   b. "Hilton"   c. title:Hilton

5. You want to find a recipe for apple pie.
   a. "pie recipe apple"   b. apple pie recipe   c. apple -pie recipe

TOTAL: _____ / 50 points

TEST 2: UNITS 4-6

(A) **Match the card messages with the types of cards in the box.**
There is one more type of card than you need.
(____ / 5 points)

a. wedding	**c.** bon voyage	**e.** thank you
b. get well	**d.** good luck	**f.** happy birthday

1. ____ I appreciate and will never forget all of your kind help.

2. ____ Wishing you lots of success! We'll keep our fingers crossed for you!

3. ____ Hope you have a great time in Hawaii!

4. ____ May you enjoy a wonderful day and another year full of nice surprises.

5. ____ You are perfect for each other. May you have a life of happiness and love.

(B) **Imagine today is your teacher's birthday. Fill out the form to send**
a birthday card to your teacher's E-mail address (or use
myteacher@mailbox.com).
(____ / 10 points)

Fill out the form below to personalize this card
"It's Your Big Day!" by Karen

Recipient's name: Recipient's E-mail address:

TO: [_____]   [_____]

Your name: Your E-mail address:

FROM: [_____]   [_____]

Click on Preview button (below) after entering messages:
You may click in the spaces below to personalize your card:

Happy Birthday!

PLEASE SELECT MUSIC BELOW
○ "Rock Around the Clock" (Playing)   ○ "Happy Birthday"

You may also enter an optional personal message here:

C **Answer the following questions about yourself.** (2 points each)   (_____ / 10 points)

1. If you could study abroad, where would you study?
   _____

2. What course would you take?
   _____

3. How long would you study?
   _____

4. What kind of accommodations would you choose?
   _____

5. What would you like to do in your free time?
   _____

D **Read the following passage about a famous person and then answer the questions below.**   (_____ / 10 points)

Bill Gates is the chief executive officer (CEO) of Microsoft Corporation. He was born on October 28, 1955, in Seattle, Washington, in the United States and grew up there. He attended a public elementary school and the private Lakeside School. There, he began programming computers at age 13. In 1973, Gates entered Harvard University as a freshman. While at Harvard, Gates created a computer language, BASIC. In 1975, he started Microsoft and, in his junior year, he dropped out of Harvard. Microsoft went on to become the most successful software company in the world, and Bill Gates became the richest man in the world. In 1995, Gates wrote *The Road Ahead,* a book explaining his ideas about computer technology and the future. Gates uses the money he makes from selling the book to help teachers worldwide who are using computers in their classrooms. He was married on January 1, 1994, to Melinda French Gates. They have one child, Jennifer Katharine Gates, born in 1996. Gates loves to read and enjoys playing golf and bridge.

1. Who is the famous person? _____

2. What does he do? _____

3. When was he born? _____

4. Where did he grow up? _____

5. When did he enter university? _____

6. What is the title of his book? _____

7. What does he do with the money he makes from selling the book?
   _____

8. What is his wife's name?

   _____

9. What is his daughter's name?

   _____

10. What are his interests?

   _____

E **Unscramble the conversations. Write a number from 1 to 5 in front of each sentence in the order you think is correct.**   ____ / 10 points

CONVERSATION 1

_____ A: I like his movies, too.

_____ B: I think he's really handsome and I like his movies.

_____ B: Mel Gibson. Do you know him?

_____ A: Who is your favorite actor?

_____ A: Yes, I do. Why is he your favorite?

CONVERSATION 2

_____ B: I like Winona Ryder best.

_____ A: I think so, too.

_____ B: She is really cool and very talented.

_____ A: What do you like about her?

_____ A: Do you have a favorite actress?

F **Choose the correct word or phrase for each sentence.**   ____ / 5 points

1. He _____ to New York when he was 20 years old.

   a. moved   **b.** might move

2. She gave a concert _____ .

   a. next month   **b.** last year

3. I _____ go sightseeing tomorrow.

   a. think I'll   **b.** maybe

4. We visited the States _____ years ago.

   a. last   **b.** three

5. Tina and Chris have been together for a year. They will _____ get married.

   a. probably   **b.** might

TOTAL: ____ / 50 points

Name _____ Date _____

TEST 3: UNITS 7-9

(A) **Match the food items on the left with the countries on the right.**   ____ / 5 points

1. _d_ kimchee   **a.** China
2. ____ sushi   **b.** India
3. ____ pizza   **c.** America
4. ____ hamburger and fries   **d.** Korea
5. ____ tandoori chicken **e.** Italy
6. ____ dim sum   **f.** Japan

(B) **Write the prices in words.** (2 points each)   ____ / 10 points

1. $25.40 _twenty-five dollars and forty cents_____
2. $69.95 _____
3. $258 _____
4. $76.50 _____
5. $125 _____
6. $12.99 _____

(C) **Answer the following questions about yourself.** (2 points each)   ____ / 10 points

1. What is the best action movie you have ever seen?

_____

2. What's your favorite science fiction movie?

_____

3. What do you think of horror movies?

_____

4. Do you like comedies?

_____

5. What's a movie you found really boring?

_____

D   **Imagine you are going shopping online. Write down ten things you can buy for the three categories in the chart.**   ____ / 10 points

Clothes & Accessories	Sports & Fitness Equipment	Electronic Equipment
a.	e.	h.
b.	f.	i.
c.	g.	j.
d.		

E   **Unscramble the conversation. Write a number from 1 to 10 in front of each sentence in the order you think is correct.**   ____ / 10 points

_____   CUSTOMER: Well-done, please.

_____   WAITER: Anything else?

_____   WAITER: Would you like anything to drink?

_____   CUSTOMER: Yes, I am.

_____   CUSTOMER: I'll have the T-bone steak with salad.

_____   CUSTOMER: Yes. I'd like a glass of red wine.

_____   WAITER: What would you like?

_____   WAITER: How would you like your steak?

_____   WAITER: Are you ready to order, sir?

_____   CUSTOMER: That'll be all. Thank you.

F   **Choose the correct word or phrase for each sentence.**   ____ / 5 points

1. I saw "Star Wars" last night! It's the best _____ I've ever seen.

   a. science fiction movie   **b.** love story

2. "Lethal Weapon 4" is an action movie. I heard it's very _____ .

   a. exciting   **b.** sad

3. I feel like a _____ . Let's watch "Dumb and Dumber." I heard it's really funny.

   a. comedy   **b.** horror movie

4. I don't like horror movies. They are really _____ .

   a. scary   **b.** scared

5. "The Matrix" is a _____ movie. I didn't understand it.

   a. wonderful   **b.** weird

TOTAL: ____ / 50 points

TEST 4: UNITS 10-13

(A) **Answer the following questions about skills and personal qualities.**
(2 points each)

1. Use words or phrases from the box below to write two skills and two personal qualities for each occupation.

friendly, polite	cooking, carving	creative, energetic
painting, drawing	reliable, hardworking	serving food, speaking foreign languages

   a. **Flight attendant**   Skills _____

      Personal qualities _____

   b. **Cook's helper**   Skills _____

      Personal qualities _____

   c. **Children's art teacher**   Skills _____

      Personal qualities _____

2. Now write down three of your skills and personal qualities.

   a. I am good at _____

   b. I can _____

   c. I am _____

(B) **Answer the following questions about cyber cafes.**

1. What is a cyber cafe?

   a. a virtual coffee shop

   b. a Web page

   c. a coffee shop with computers connected to the Internet

2. Write five activities you can do at a cyber cafe.

   a. _____

   b. _____

   c. _____

   d. _____

   e. _____

3. Have you ever visited a cyber cafe before? If yes, where and when?

   _____

C **Describe your ideal vacation.** (2 points each) (___ / 12 points)

1. Which place would you visit?
   _____

2. What accommodations would you choose?
   _____

3. How long would you stay there?
   _____

4. What activities would you do?
   _____

5. Would you go there alone or with friends?
   _____

6. Why is this your ideal vacation?
   _____

D **Read the following news story and then answer the questions.** (___ / 6 points)

76-Year-Old Woman Wins Millions in the State Lottery

CALIFORNIA – A 76-year-old Los Angeles woman was last week's winner of the $4 million in the State Lottery drawing.

Mrs. Patricia Miles, a former kindergarten teacher, got the lottery ticket from her husband as a birthday present. "I've never won anything in my whole life," she said, after she learned the exciting news. "It's a miracle!" Mrs. Miles was having breakfast with her husband, Ralph, when he read the winning number from the newspaper. They immediately rushed to the lottery offices to present the winning ticket.

Miles, who has five children and twelve grandchildren, promised to take her whole family on a cruise to the Caribbean. With the rest of the money, Miles plans to make a large donation to St. John's Children's Hospital, where she has been a volunteer aid for the last ten years. She said, "I love children, and now I am happy to be able to help them even more."

1. What is the name of the winner of the State Lottery drawing?
   _____

2. How old is she?
   _____

3. Where is she from?
   _____

4. Who gave her the lottery ticket?

_____

5. How many children and grandchildren does she have?

_____

6. Where did she promise to take her whole family?

_____

(E) **Write down the correct job for each sentence.**   _____ / 10 points

1. A s <u>k i i n s t r u c t o r</u> works at Alpine resorts.

2. A n _ _ _ _ takes care of little kids and works in private homes.

3. A c _ _ _ works in restaurant kitchens.

4. A l _ _ _ _ _ _ _ _ _ works at beaches and swimming pools.

5. An o _ _ _ _ _ w _ _ _ _ _ works in an office. (2 points)

6. A t _ _ _ _ _ _ _ _ _ _ _ _ sells things over the telephone.

7. A f _ _ _ _ _ _ a _ _ _ _ _ _ _ _ serves food on airplanes. (2 points)

8. A c _ _ _ _ c _ _ _ _ _ _ _ _ _ works at summer camps. (2 points)

TOTAL: _____ / 50 points

Internet English Tests
Answer Key

TEST 1: Units 1-3

A.

1. d	7. i
2. h	8. k
3. e	9. c
4. j	10. f
5. g	11. a
6. b	

B. *Answers will vary.*

C. *Answers will vary.*

D.

1. The Internet is a network of millions of computers.
2. They are linked together by phone lines, fiberoptic cables, satellite, and microwave connections.
3. The United States Department of Defense started the Internet in 1969.
4. Nobody owns it.
5. WWW stands for World Wide Web.
6. A typical Web page looks like a magazine page.
7. When you click on a link you go to a new Web page.
8. The most popular part of the Internet is the World Wide Web.
9. The two most popular Web browsers are Netscape Navigator™ and Internet Explorer™.
10. *Any two of the following answers:* send E-mail; go shopping; find jobs; get the latest news; order a meal; make travel plans.

E.
9 / 10 / 5 / 1 / 6 / 2 / 11 / 3 / 8 / 7 / 4

F.

1. b	4. c
2. c	5. b
3. a	

TEST 2: Units 4-6

A.

1. e
2. d
3. c
4. f
5. a

B. *Answers will vary.*

C. *Answers will vary.*

D.

1. The famous person is Bill Gates.
2. He is the chief executive officer of Microsoft Corporation.
3. He was born in Seattle, Washington, in the United States.
4. He grew up in Seattle, Washington, in the United States.
5. He entered university in 1973.
6. The title of his book is *The Road Ahead*.
7. He gives the money to teachers worldwide who are using computers in their classroom.
8. His wife's name is Melinda French Gates.
9. His daughter's name is Jennifer Katharine Gates.
10. He loves to read and enjoys playing golf and bridge.

E.
CONVERSATION 1
5 / 4 / 2 / 1 / 3

CONVERSATION 2
2 / 5 / 4 / 3 / 1

F.

1. a	4. b
2. b	5. a
3. a	

A.
1. d
2. f
3. e
4 c
5. b
6. a

B.
1. twenty-five dollars and forty cents
2. sixty-nine dollars and ninety-five cents
3. two hundred fifty-eight dollars
4. seventy-six dollars and fifty cents
5. one hundred twenty-five dollars
6. twelve dollars and ninety-nine cents

C. *Answers will vary.*

D. *Answers will vary.*

E.
6 / 9 / 7 / 2 / 4 / 8 / 3 / 5 / 1 / 10

F.
1. a
2. a
3. a
4. a
5. b

A.
1. a. **Flight attendant**
   Skills: serving food, speaking foreign languages
   Personal qualities: friendly, polite
   b. **Cook's helper**
   Skills: cooking, carving
   Personal qualities: reliable, hardworking
   c. **Children's art teacher**
   Skills: painting, drawing
   Personal qualities: creative, energetic
2. *Answers will vary.*

B.
1. c
2. *Answers will vary.*
3. *Answers will vary.*

C. *Answers will vary.*

D.
1. Her name is Mrs. Patricia Miles.
2. She is 76 years old.
3. She is from Los Angeles.
4. Her husband gave her the lottery ticket.
5. She has five children and twelve grandchildren.
6. She promised to take her whole family on a cruise to the Caribbean.

E.
1. ski instructor
2. nanny
3. cook
4. lifeguard
5. office worker
6. telemarketer
7. flight attendant
8. camp counselor

Internet English Vocabulary Log

Why Use a Vocabulary Log

The *Vocabulary Log* can be introduced in order to draw students' attention to new vocabulary items and phrases that they are likely to come across during their Web searches. It consists of five vocabulary cards that allow each student to create a personalized list of words that he/she would like to know. Keeping personalized notes on a set of words or phrases can motivate students to enrich their vocabulary. In addition, choosing words or phrases as they naturally occur on the Web raises student awareness of words in collocation rather than in isolation.

Preparation

1. Make a copy of the *Vocabulary Log* (page 98) for each student. The sheet contains five cards to be used with each *Web Search* unit (Units 4–13) in the **Student Book.** Depending on your students' level of English, you can give them more vocabulary cards (i.e., make two or more copies of the *Vocabulary Log* sheet per student).

2. Ask students to have the *Vocabulary Log* with them when they carry out their Web search.

3. Tell students to choose five words or phrases they are unfamiliar with and write each word or phrase on a separate card. In each unit, you can ask students to select vocabulary that is directly related to the topic of the unit. For example:

   Unit 4: interests, family information, career history

   Unit 5: card greetings

   Unit 6: course types, social activities, school descriptions

   Unit 7: different types of food

   Unit 8: clothes, accessories, sports and fitness equipment, electronic equipment

   Unit 9: types of movies, plot summaries, settings

   Unit 10: activities, attractions, hotel facilities

   Unit 11: food, drinks, hardware, software

   Unit 12: jobs, job descriptions, job skills, personal qualities

   Unit 13: various vocabulary in news story headlines

Guidelines

- Encourage students to write down phrases they find on the Web rather than individual words to raise their awareness of words in collocation.

- For each word or phrase students should write down its meaning in English and/or in their native language, and an example of use. The example can be taken directly from the Web.

- Allow students to use their dictionaries (English-English or bilingual) or alternatively use the following online dictionaries:

   http://www.dictionary.com/

   http://www.facstaff.bucknell.edu/rbeard/diction. html

Vocabulary Activities

There are different vocabulary activities you can carry out with the vocabulary cards depending on the level of your students and the time available. For example:

- Pairs of students can exchange cards and then ask each other the meaning and an example of use for the words or phrases. This can be done in person or by E-mail.

- Students can teach each other the meaning of the words or phrases and show each other the Web pages where they found them.

- After teaching each other their words or phrases, the cards can be individually cut out and placed in a hat. A student can pick one out at random and ask a classmate to guess the meaning from the example of the word or phrase in context.

Teachers who create other interesting uses for the vocabulary cards are invited to share their ideas with other teachers at the *Internet English Website:*

   http://www.oup.com/elt/internet.english

Vocabulary Log

1. Choose five words or phrases that you are unfamiliar with.
2. Write them in the cards provided (one word or phrase per card).
3. Use a dictionary to find the meaning of each word or phrase.
4. Write an example of use for each word or phrase.

Vocabulary Card

Word/Phrase: _____

Meaning: _____

Example: _____

Vocabulary Card

Word/Phrase: _____

Meaning: _____

Example: _____

Vocabulary Card

Word/Phrase: _____

Meaning: _____

Example: _____

Vocabulary Card

Word/Phrase: _____

Meaning: _____

Example: _____

Vocabulary Card

Word/Phrase: _____

Meaning: _____

Example: _____

Teaching Basic HTML for Web Pages

Why Create a Web Page

Helping students publish an English-language homepage on the Internet is very rewarding:

- It gives students a sense of achievement.
- Students are involved in the latest era of Web publishing.
- It helps students practice their English-language skills and be creative at the same time.
- It can help students find keypals.
- It motivates students to continue working even outside class time.

Starting Out

There is a lot of Web publishing software available on the market and some applications can be downloaded free from the Internet. If you have experience using a particular application for creating Web pages then it is a good idea to show your students how to use the application for creating their homepages. However, if you have not used Web publishing software before, this handout will show you and your students how to construct a homepage using a small number of basic HTML tags and a basic word processor.

HTML (HyperText Mark-up Language)

The basic language of Web page design is the HyperText Mark-up Language (HTML). HTML is very simple and basic, and it consists of *tags* (usually abbreviations of English words in brackets). For example, <B> stands for **Bold** <I> stands for *Italics*, <FONT> stands for Font. There are *opening tags*, e.g., <B>, *closing tags*, e.g., </B>, and *stand alone tags*, e.g., <P>.

Students can compose their homepages using any basic text editor (e.g., SimpleText, Wordpad, or Notepad) or word processor (e.g., Microsoft Word, Claris Works, WordPerfect).

There are many advantages to composing a Web page in HTML:

- Students don't have to use complicated software.
- They become aware of how Web pages work.
- They can utilize the format of other Web pages that are already published on the Web (i.e., they can view the HTML source and see how the pages are constructed).

How to Teach HTML

Use the handouts to show students exactly what to do (*see Introduction to HTML*, pages 101–106). With each new tag that is introduced, students are shown exactly how it works by a clear example (e.g., making a rollercoaster,[1] making a birthday wish list). Students type the given example into a text file at their computer. When students finish typing in the example, they can view the result by opening their Web browser and selecting their file to view. In this way students will learn all the HTML tags they need to create a Web page. After they feel comfortable with the basic HTML tags, they can start creating their own homepage.

What to Include in a Homepage

Depending on your students' level of English, you can ask students to include information that will help them utilize whatever they have learned in their English classes. For example, here are some ideas:

- A self-introduction (name, age, birthday, hobbies, hometown, family, etc.)
- Information (and links) about their school
- Their favorites (movie star, musician, movie, food recipe, vacation destination, etc.), including links to their favorite websites
- Plans for the future (dream job, car, house, etc.)
- Vacation experiences (places they visited or would like to visit, things they liked, etc.)

Finally, ask students to add their E-mail address for prospective keypals.

---

[1] See Joe Barta's website for more HTML activities: http://apk.net~jbarta/tutor/makapage/

Introduction to HTML

PART 1

In this part you will learn some of the basic *HTML tags* **that will help you put together a homepage in English.**

To create the HTML files you will need to use a text editor or word processor. To view your files you will need to use a Web browser.

- Turn on your computer.
- Open your text editor or word processor.
- Now you are ready to start typing your HTML code.
- Type:

```
<HTML>
</HTML>
```

What you have just typed are called *tags*. <HTML> is an example of an *opening tag*. </HTML> is an example of a *closing tag*. *Tags* are always enclosed in brackets like these: < >. To make a closing tag just add a / to the starting tag.

With tags you give instructions to the computer. <HTML> tells the computer that this is the start of an HTML document, and <HTML> tells the computer that this is the end of an HTML document.

Now you can add some more things to the homepage. Every HTML document needs a pair of <HEAD> tags, <TITLE> tags and <BODY> tags. The rest of your homepage is going to be within the <BODY> tags.

- Type:

```
<HTML>
<HEAD>
<TITLE> </TITLE>
</HEAD>
<BODY>
</BODY>
</HTML>
```

- Now you can give your document a title:

```
<HTML>
<HEAD>
<TITLE>Mika's Homepage</TITLE>
</HEAD>
<BODY>
</BODY>
</HTML>
```

- Now you need to **Save** your file **As**: *index.html* (or *index.htm*). Place your file into a folder with your name as the title.

To view your homepage:

- Open your Web browser.
- In *Netscape* select **Open** from the **File** menu then select **Page in Navigator**. In *Internet Explorer* select **Open File...**
- In the new window, find your index.html (or index.htm) file and click **Open**.

Each time you make a change to your HTML file, you need to save it and then view it with your Web browser. Make sure to save word processor files as unformatted *text only* files.

PART 2

In this part you will learn how to use Bold, *Italics,* <u>Underline</u>**, as well as different fonts and sizes.**

- Open your HTML document.
- Between the <BODY> tags, type a sentence (for example: This is my homepage).
- Use the <B> tags to make the word "my" bold.

```
<BODY>
This is <B>my</B> homepage.
</BODY>
```

- Now use the <I> tags for italics:

```
<BODY>
This <I>is</I><B> my</B> homepage.
</BODY>
```

- Use the **<U>** tags for underlining:

```
<BODY>
<U>This </U><I>is</I>
<B> my</B> homepage.
</BODY>
```

- You can use tags in combination as well:

```
<BODY>
This is <I><B> my</B></I> homepage.
</BODY>
```

Now you can use different fonts and sizes.

- First add the <FONT> tags:

```
<BODY>
This is my <FONT>homepage.</FONT>
</BODY>
```

- Then specify a **SIZE** *attribute*:

```
<BODY>
This is my <FONT SIZE=6>
homepage.</FONT>
</BODY>
```

A tag tells the browser to do something. An *attribute* goes inside the tag brackets and tells the browser how to do it. So <FONT> is a tag, SIZE is an attribute.

Fonts come in 7 sizes:

1 — smallest	5 — large
2 — very small	6 — very large
3 — small	7 — largest
4 — medium	

Now try and make a rollercoaster!

- Between the <BODY> tags type:

```
r<FONT SIZE=4>o</FONT>
<FONT SIZE=4>l</FONT>
<FONT SIZE=5>l</FONT>
<FONT SIZE=6>e</FONT>
<FONT SIZE=7>r</FONT>
<FONT SIZE=7>c</FONT>
<FONT SIZE=6>o</FONT>
<FONT SIZE=5>a</FONT>
<FONT SIZE=4>s</FONT>
<FONT SIZE=3>t</FONT>
<FONT SIZE=2>e</FONT>
<FONT SIZE=1>r!</FONT>
```

You can also choose a different font (e.g., Times, Arial, Geneva):

```
<BODY>
This is my <U><I><B>
<FONT FACE="TIMES"
SIZE="7">homepage</FONT> </B></I></U>
</BODY>
```

PART 3

In this part you will learn how to change the background color of your homepage, as well as the color of your text and links.

When you create a homepage, your browser automatically makes the background color gray. But gray is not very pretty. So here is how to change it.

- Type:

```
<BODY BGCOLOR="#FFFFFF">
This is my homepage.
</BODY>
```

#FFFFFF is computer language for white. To view more background colors go to this website: **http://www.infi.net/wwwimages/colorindex.html** Try a few different background colors and choose the one you like the most for your homepage. You can also use a standard color name, e.g., WHITE, BLUE, RED, instead of the computer color codes.

Here is how to change the color of the text.

- Type:

```
<BODY TEXT="#000000">
</BODY>
```

This produces a page with black text because the color code #000000 is the code for black. Now try different colors for your text to match your background color.

Here is how to change the color of a single word in your text.

- Type:

```
<BODY BGCOLOR="#FFFFFF">
This is <FONT COLOR="#FF0000">
my</FONT> homepage.
</BODY>
```

Here is how to change the font, color, and size of a word.

- Type:

```
<BODY BGCOLOR="#FFFFFF">
This is my <FONT COLOR="#FF0000"
FACE="ARIAL" SIZE="7">homepage.</FONT>
</BODY>
```

PART 4

In this part you will learn how to use breaks and spaces.

When you want to insert line breaks into your homepage, you can use the <BR> tag.

- Type:

```
<BODY BGCOLOR="#FFFFFF">
This<BR>is<BR>my<BR>homepage.
</BODY>
```

- Similar to <BR> is <P>. It does exactly the same thing, but after the line break it skips a line:

```
<BODY BGCOLOR="#FFFFFF">
This<P>is<P>my<P>homepage.
</BODY>
```


 and <P> are examples of *stand alone tags. They do not need a closing tag.* Also, you cannot use them more than once in a row. For example, if you type <P><P><P> it won't give you three empty lines, it will just give you one empty line.

- If you want more than one space between words, type:

```
<BODY BGCOLOR="#FFFFFF">
Hi!    This is my homepage.
</BODY>
```

  is a special computer code that means **"non-breaking space"** to the browser. Here are some other codes for special characters:

& (& ampersand)
" (" quotation mark)
¥ (¥ yen sign)

PART 5

In this part you will learn how to make lists.

There are *ordered lists* and *unordered lists.*

This is an *ordered list:*

1. something old
2. something new
3. something borrowed
4. something blue

This is an *unordered list:*

- something old
- something new
- something borrowed
- something new

First, try making an *unordered list.*

- Type:

```
<BODY>
What I want for my birthday
</BODY>
```

- Add a pair of **Unordered List** tags:

```
<BODY>
What I want for my birthday
<UL>
</UL>
</BODY>
```

- Add a **List Item:**

```
<BODY>
What I want for my birthday
<UL>
<LI>thirty red roses
</UL>
</BODY>
```

- Add a few more **List Items:**

```
<BODY>
What I want for my birthday
<UL>
<LI>thirty red roses
<LI>a new T-shirt
<LI>a bag
<LI>a pair of shoes
</UL>
</BODY>
```

Here is how to make an *ordered list*.
Change the <UL> tag to <OL>:

```
<BODY>
What I want for my birthday
<OL>
<LI>thirty red roses
<LI>a new T-shirt
<LI>a bag
<LI>a pair of shoes
</OL>
</BODY>
```

PART 6

In this part you will learn how to make links to websites and to your E-mail address.

Here is how to make a link to Yahoo!
- First type this:

```
<BODY>
Go to Yahoo!
</BODY>
```

- Then add a pair of Anchor tags:

```
<BODY>
Go to <A>Yahoo!</A>
</BODY>
```

- Finally, add the URL address:

```
<BODY>
Go to <A
HREF="http://www.yahoo.com/"> Yahoo!</A>
</BODY>
```

Here is how to add a link to your E-mail address.
- Type:

```
<BODY>
Send me <A
HREF="mailto:YOUR@EMAIL.ADDRESS">
Mail!</A>
</BODY>
```

PART 7

In this part you will learn how to use a horizontal rule.

- To create a horizontal rule in your homepage, type:

```
<BODY>
<HR>
</BODY>
```

- You can change the width of the horizontal rule. Try these:

```
<BODY>
<HR WIDTH=20>
<HR WIDTH=50>
<HR WIDTH=100>
</BODY>
```

- You can choose whether you want the rule on the left, in the center, or on the right:

```
<BODY>
<HR WIDTH=20 ALIGN=LEFT>
<HR WIDTH=50 ALIGN=RIGHT>
<HR WIDTH=100 ALIGN=CENTER>
</BODY>
```

PART 8

In this part you will learn how to create tables.

There are several new tags you will need to learn:

<TABLE>...</TABLE>
This tells the computer to create a table.

The next three are attributes for a table. You can choose their size (1–8):
BORDER is the size of the border of the table.
CELLPADDING changes the size of the cells.
CELLSPACING changes the distance between the cells.

<TR>...</TR>
These tags are for starting and ending rows in a table.

<TH>...</TH>
Use these tags around a table header, which is a title for a column or row.

<TD>...</TD>
The content of each single cell in your table needs to be enclosed by these tags.

- Now try making some tables. You can make different types of tables. Here is a table with titles along the top:

```
<TABLE BORDER=6CELLPADDING=6
CELLSPACING=6>
<TR><TH>Actors</TH>
<TH>Movies</TH></TR>
<TR><TD>Brad Pitt</TD>
<TD>Seven</TD></TR>
<TR><TD>Mel Gibson</TD>
<TD>Lethal Weapon</TD></TR>
</TABLE>
```

When you are finished, it should look like this:

Actors	Movies
Brad Pitt	Seven
Mel Gibson	Lethal Weapon

Here is how to create a table that has titles down the side:

```
<TABLE BORDER=6 CELLPADDING=6
CELLSPACING=6>
<TR><TH>Actors</TH>
<TD>Brad Pitt</TD>
<TD>Mel Gibson</TD></TR>
<TR><TH>Movies</TH>
<TD>Seven</TD>
<TD>Lethal Weapon</TD></TR>
</TABLE>
```

When you are finished, it should look like this:

Actors	Brad Pitt	Mel Gibson
Movies	Seven	Lethal Weapon

It is also possible to make a table that has one header across more than one row by using the **COLSPAN** attribute with the **<TH>** tag:

```
<TABLE BORDER=6 CELLPADDING=6
CELLSPACING=6>
<TR><TH COLSPAN=2>
My Favorite...</TH></TR>
<TR> <TD>Actor</TD>
<TD>Brad Pitt</TD></TR>
<TR><TD>Movie</TD>
<TD>Seven</TD></TR>
</TABLE>
```

When you are finished, it should look like this:

My Favorite...	
Actor	Brad Pitt
Movie	Seven

PART 9

If you want to add your photo to your homepage, you will need to take your picture with a digital camera or scan your picture. Save the picture file in *GIF* or *JPEG* format. For example, you can save it as *yourpicture.GIF*. You can then add your photo to your homepage.

- Type:

```
<IMG SRC="yourpicture.GIF">
```

You can put your photo on the left, on the right or in the center.

- Type:

```
<IMG SRC="yourpicture.GIF"
ALIGN=LEFT>
<IMG SRC="yourpicture.GIF"
ALIGN=RIGHT>
<IMG SRC="yourpicture.GIF"
ALIGN=CENTER>
```

Now you can start creating your own homepage!

USEFUL LINKS
Here is a list of websites that offer step-by-step HTML lessons:
http://apk.net/~jbarta/tutor/makapage/
http://www.hotwired.com/webmonkey/kids/
http://www.edb.utexas.edu/resta97/aisd/students/turnbull/HTMLtutr/index.html
http://www-ssg.sr.unh.edu/tof/WebLesson/web_lesson.html
http://204.98.1.2/high/awest/learnhtml/00conten.htm
http://www.hollandcomputers.com/Internet_services/html.htm